CHAMPIONS ARE RAISED, NOT BORN

CHAMPIONS ARE RAISED, NOT BORN

HOW MY PARENTS MADE ME A SUCCESS

SUMMER SANDERS
WITH **MELINDA MARSHALL**

DELACORTE PRESS

Published by
Delacorte Press
Random House, Inc.
1540 Broadway
New York, New York 10036

Library of Congress Catloging-in-Publication Data

Sanders, Summer.
Champions are raised, not born : how my parents made me a success / by Summer Sanders with Melinda Marshall.
p. cm.
ISBN 0-385-33421-4
1. Sanders, Summer.   2. Swimmers—United States Biography.
3. Women swimmers—United States Biography.   4. Parent and child—United States.   I. Marshall, Melinda M., 1961–   .   II. Title.
GV838.S33A3   1999
797.2′1′092—dc21
[B]   99-22003
CIP

Manufactured in the United States of America
Published simultaneously in Canada

July 1999

10 9 8 7 6 5 4 3 2 1

BVG

FOR MOM AND POPS

and

in Memory of Grandpa Charlie and my "superfriend"

ACKNOWLEDGMENTS

There are so many people to thank—for helping me write this book, for supporting me all along the way, and for always being there.

In my family: Bob Sanders, Barbara Hopewell, Trevor Sanders, Danielle Sanders, Jeremy Sanders, Jenni Sanders, Ryder Sanders, Rick Sanders, Johanna Sanders, Elaine Sanders, Charlie Sanders, Dawn and Keith Hopewell, Steve Slagel, Bob and Nancy Wanek, Mark Henderson, Marty and Maryann Henderson, Paul Henderson, Curley Wurley, Gorgeous Jeanne, and my dogs, Smalls and Tahoe.

Of my coaches: Ralph Thomas, Mike Hastings, Richard Quick, Ross Gerry, and Jonty Skinner.

Of my friends: Heidi Eick, Heather McClurg, Meghan Pattyson, Nicole Haislett, Janie Wagstaff, Peff and Nikki Eick, Bill and Mikki McClurg, Gentry Lee, Mary and Ron Thompson, Collette Thompson, Richard Diana, Seth Mayeri, Michael Glantz, Helen Broder, Parkes Brittan, Susy Westfall, Dan Jansen, Bonnie Blair, Norm Bellingham, Karch Kiraly, Debbie Thomas, Dot Richardson, Justin Huish, Matt Biondi, and Melinda Marshall.

I'd also like to thank War Crew, Sugar Bears, California Capital Aquatics, Sierra Aquatic Club, Stanford Swimming, U.S. Swimming, and Oakmont High School.

CONTENTS

INTRODUCTION

Champions Are Raised, Not Born

What's the measure of your success as a parent? A kid who beats all the pros before he's a teenager? Who grows up to command an audience of millions? Who's worth a billion dollars before he's thirty?

I'm writing this book to suggest a different standard, a better measure of successful parenting: a child who consistently gives all she's got with what she's been given. A child who feels capable and enthusiastic, no matter what the challenge. A child who arrives at adulthood with a skill or sport or talent that will give her satisfaction the rest of her life. A child who does what she sets out to do, but doesn't quit there. A child for whom satisfaction is in the doing, not the getting.

The Olympics, thanks to my parents, never were my destination. They never were the end that would justify any means or any sacrifice. They were almost an accident, a by-product, a career perk. I'd started swimming because my family had a pool;

I'd started competing because I wanted to be with my brother, Trevor, and his friends; I'd kept going to practice because my friends were there, and because we went on fun trips; and suddenly, when I was fifteen, I stumbled on the proof that I was really good at this—good enough to make an Olympic team, good enough to be someday the very best, if only for a brief period.

My parents never saw my talent or my competitive drive as an invitation to impose any ambitions on me. They were never in it for the medals on the wall. All they ever wanted was for me to be happy—secure, well-liked, well-rounded. They did not put a pool in our backyard to make me into a champion; whatever I wanted to do, they were behind me, matching their level of commitment to mine. They did not handpick the activities of my childhood and adolescence with an eye to grooming me for greatness; a sense of security and strong family ties were what they aimed to give me. They did not ship me off to swimming camp, or to another family, or to a celebrity coach so that I might have a better shot at world records; they didn't take me out of school or any of the social activities that revolved around school.

Just the opposite, in fact. My dad was on a constant campaign to keep my sport in the background. He loved to quote Mae West, whose motto was "Life's a party, only most damn fools don't know they're invited." He made sure I had fun—with him and my brother, with my friends, with school, with vacations, with prom dates and part-time jobs, with movies and pizza parties. My mom, too, recognized that there was more to life than a fifty-meter pool lane: her job, as she saw it, was to give me the grounding to weather any ups and downs, in any arena, mostly by ensuring I had a consistent home life. My parents never lost sight of their job as parents, which was to make sure I grew up carefree but responsible, educated and athletic, confident and capable of going after whatever it was that I dreamed about. Swimming was a means to all those things, not an end in itself.

And they did their job really, really well, because I love what I am doing today, getting better at it all the time—and because from the age of four, I did something I loved until I did it better than anybody else.

What might make their accomplishment even more amazing to some is the fact that my parents were divorced for most of my childhood. In fact, I can't remember them ever being married: they split for good when I was seven and my brother, Trevor, was nine. For the next ten years, Trevor and I split the year between them. Every October, we'd move into Mom's house and every April, we'd go back to the house and swimming pool and sport court that my parents had built together and where my dad continued to live. It helped that both my parents chose to stay in the same school district, so that we didn't have to switch schools and friends, and so that we could celebrate birthdays together. But my parents were never my parents at the same time, not as a unit.

People who don't know me are often shocked at this piece of news. Divorce and dysfunction, they go together. But divorce and achievement? Divorce and self-esteem? Success out of failure? There's something so all-American, so wholesome, about the Olympics that to some it doesn't seem possible anyone who participates in them, let alone wins a couple of gold medals, could come from a broken home. A lot of people expect kids

3

whose parents split up to have had a crummy childhood. Too many people assume that parents who fail at marriage must also fail at parenting.

I can understand that. I'd never want to gloss over the horrors of divorce, I'd never want to imply that it was the right thing to do, or the best thing for us, because it wasn't: it was the worst thing, it totally sucked. Those two days of every year that we made the switch, from one parent's house to the other, were the most painful of my existence—like having my heart torn out and put in a blender. But by and large, Trevor and I had a happy childhood, one we wouldn't go back and change even if we could. Many positive things grew out of my parents' divorce. I think my mom and dad, because they failed each other, were all the more committed to not failing us. Despite or because of their single-parent situation, they gave my brother and me the kind of grounding, the kind of support, the kind of unconditional love many other parents, even those married, somehow fail to provide.

Of course, neither my mom nor my dad would presume to tell anybody how to parent. They wouldn't dare write this book. (Who would ever want to hear child-rearing advice from a divorced parent?) I think they're not entirely sure what affected us so profoundly, other than the divorce. I think they look at Trevor and me and say, "We're so blessed to have such terrific kids"—as though it were a surprise.

But I see their role very clearly now, and it was anything but passive. And because they can't or won't or shouldn't be the ones to describe it, I must. That's why this is not just another Olympic athlete memoir. It's intended to be an account of successful parenting from the product's viewpoint, which parents almost never get to read these days, since it's the fashion to blame parents for every disappointment and failure experienced so far. My mom and dad deserve to be recognized for the job they did, not because I won gold medals and set records, but because the person I aspired to become, growing up, is the person I've grown up to be. They gave me what so many men and women miss out on: the infinite satisfaction and self-confidence that comes from getting to do what you do best and knowing you're tapping your potential to the fullest.

I want to share just how they did it, because ever since I've gone on the road, speaking to kids and their parents about the importance of sports, that's what people want to know. Over and over, I get the same questions: *When did they recognize your talent? What did they do then? How did they motivate you? How did they get you to stick with it?*

So many of these parents have the wrong idea. So many of them are caught up in this obsession with Singular Talent. They've read Earl Woods's account of taming the Tiger with a golf club from the age of two. They've heard how Andre Agassi's father put a racket in his son's hand when he was barely three years old. They've seen all those NBC segments on gymnasts who grow up in another state with coaches for parents. They've got this idea that child rearing is a science, not an art, a serious mission with nothing left to chance or a child's inclination.

They're missing the whole point of parenthood.

I'm not trying to discredit what the parents of prodigies have accomplished—not at all. But when a mother comes up to me at a mall and says, pointing to her kid, "*She's* going to the 2004 Olympics," I want to sit that mother down and set her straight.

I want her to understand that the only thing that'll take her daughter to the furthest edge of her potential is the sheer pleasure she takes in exercising her God-given ability. I want to talk to her about the true nature of motivation—how it's sparked by doing something fun, how it builds from doing something well, but how it can be snuffed out by parents who are too pushy, who are focused on the product rather than the process. I want to show her how to be there for her child, not just by driving her to practice, but by understanding her sport and her goals and what makes her try harder. I want this mom to understand what makes a coach great—and how his job differs from hers. I want her to understand self-esteem: how confidence and mental toughness come not from being handed rewards and compliments, but from being encouraged to set goals and to go after them until they're achieved. I want her to never underestimate the importance of her role as a grounding wire, as the person who loves unconditionally and never confuses what her child does with who her child is. More than anything, I want her to see the importance of putting her child in the driver's seat—because the sooner she does, the sooner her child will understand that the trip ahead is all up to her, and that she can handle whatever's down the road herself.

I'm glad to say I'm not the only one who can share this information. Many of the Olympic athletes I know similarly credit their parents, so I've included their stories along with mine. What they tell about their growing-up years—about finding their sport, competing in it, finding satisfaction in it, winning and losing in it, and ultimately, giving it up for a new competitive outlet—both confirms and elaborates on my own experience. Our childhoods were incredibly average; our adolescent years weren't all that different from anybody else's. But we all felt our sport and our families gave us something special, something that would help us rise head and shoulders above the pack. Taken together, I think our experiences offer a pattern for parents to follow no matter where their child's talents may lie— whether in sports or academics, music or drama, chess or auto mechanics. I think the factors that encourage somebody to push themselves to achieve their personal best are the same no matter what the arena, no matter what the ability.

Getting the Big Picture

While I was competing, I couldn't have told you what those factors were, exactly. I couldn't see for myself what accounted for my own success, certainly not in terms of the big picture, because I was too busy striving to stay on top. I was, however, an expert at analyzing my success or failure in any given race; if I blew an event, I could tell you, as I told my coach, just what went wrong, just where I failed to pace correctly, just how much more efficient I could have made my turns, just when I should have put my head down instead of taking that last breath into the wall. But I was so focused on the very short term—my next meet, my next goal time—I couldn't have possibly told you how it was that I pulled ahead of the competition, consistently, predictably, from one championship to the next until I stood on that topmost Olympic medals platform.

I'd been up against some serious talent, kids who were natural athletes, kids who were born competitors. How was it, then, that so many of them faded away, never enjoying the opportunities or rewards that came my way? What accounted for their not going the final mile? How come they bowed to the intense pressure and stomach-churning nerves, whereas I fed off it? They worked hard, they had great coaches, they had natural ability, and they wanted to win. So why didn't their dreams materialize, and mine did?

I couldn't figure it out—but then, I didn't give it all that much thought, either. Not until 1996, when I went to qualify for the 1996 Olympic team that would go to the Atlanta Games. Not until I swam my best event, the 200 'fly, the event that won me my one individual gold medal in Barcelona . . . and came in eighth.

I've come to be so grateful for that failure, because it provided just the sort of understanding I needed. It forced me to review all that had brought me to that point in time, all my upbringing and training, all my meets and championships, all the faces and places I'd known through my sport, all the lessons I'd learned from my parents and from competing. And in examining and reexamining all those memories, I came away with answers to this question of how some of us get to attain our personal best, while others live out their entire lives never knowing the satisfaction of using their gifts to their utmost.

Champions are raised, not born. I absolutely believe that. Because what gave me the edge, what helped me rise above my peers, even above my own expectations—the discipline, the mental toughness, the emotional stability, and the infinite belief in my own capacity for improvement—inevitably can be traced back to my parents, to my nurture rather than my nature. Their unqualified acceptance of me and their joyful support freed me up emotionally to take risks, to not fear failure. Their insistence on personal accountability made me see myself, and myself alone, responsible for the course my swimming took—how high I reached or how hard I fell. The grounding they gave me helped me remember that no matter how much other people were counting on me to win, the only expectations I had to meet were my own, and the only people who mattered were those who loved me regardless of where I placed in a race.

The values and standards I hold, the vision I have for myself, my outlook on the world, my sense of self-worth, and my belief that I can do whatever I put my mind to—all of which my parents instilled in me while I was swimming—are what will continue to make me strive, to achieve, and to be happy and fulfilled in whatever the next set of trials may be—a career in television, marriage, children, and meaningful contribution to my community. These are the gifts of my childhood that will last the rest of my life, long after everyone's forgotten my butterfly technique, long after people remember me as a gold medalist in Barcelona in 1992.

I'm not a parent, so I'm not writing this to *tell* anybody how to be one. I am, however, hoping to *show* what my parents did right by sharing all the stories of my seventeen-year swimming career, because I put their child-rearing philosophies to the test, over and over, and didn't find any of them lacking. For me, writing this book amounts to a sort of thank-you letter—the kind I'm always tempted to write to teachers and coaches who made a big difference in my life, but somehow never do. This is a start. For parents reading this—well, I hope it will be an inspiration.

1

To Push or Not to Push:
That Is *the* Question

G o to any athletic competition, and you can't miss them.
They're the parents on the soccer field who run up and
down with the team, screaming out directives: "Get IN there
and GET THE BALL!" They're the ones at the rink shouting
through a megaphone, the ones who won't let their kid leave
the ice, even when practice is over, even when the coach has
gone home. They're the ones at an archery tournament who are
out on the field, positioning and holding the bow for their son
or daughter. They're the ones at a swim meet who are down on
their hands and knees at the end of the lane, pounding the deck
with their fists, screaming, "GO GO GO GO!" or running
alongside the pool, arms windmilling, yelling at the top of their
lungs, "Come ON! HURRY *UP*, YOU'RE FALLING BE-
HIND!!!"

At the end of the game, or the race, or the tournament, or
the performance, these are the people who, despite pouring

their guts out moments earlier, now stand tight-lipped, hands on hips, head shaking in disappointment if their child failed to win. Their kids are the ones who aren't smiling, who won't meet their parent's eyes. Their kids are the ones who either get dead silent or throw unbelievable tantrums.

My fellow athletes and I have all seen parents like these. We've all known their kid, or competed against him.

I remember this swimmer Kent, who grew up training on a team near mine, in Arden Hills (home to Mark Spitz and Debbie Meyer). When he didn't win or place in a meet, he went totally berserk. He'd cry, he'd curse, he'd scream, he'd throw his goggles and hit someone with them, he'd yell at his mom. It was awful. My mom and I used to watch in stunned amazement. His parents were such nice people; you'd never see them or hear them being out of line during a meet. However Kent must have perceived an unspoken agenda. Kent was the last in a family of swimmers—his three sisters all competed—and by the time he was nine years old, he seemed to know he was his parents' last hope of seeing a child of theirs rank among the other champions of Arden Hills. An awful lot appeared to be riding on Kent.

Parents want their children to excel. They want their child to win—of course they do. It's understandable that a parent would get worked up to a fever pitch during actual competition—the nerves, the excitement, the untapped potential gets to everybody, whether they're on the sidelines or in the action. It's natural for parents to wish their kid would beat all the other kids, if only because there's often a lot of their time and money invested in the sport. I don't think there's anything wrong with wanting your kid to be a winner, and to go on being a winner—to be, even, the very best.

But there's a huge difference between *wanting* a child to *do* her absolute best and *needing* her to *be* the absolute best. It's the difference between wanting a child to fulfill her potential and wishing she would fulfill the one you want for her. It can be the difference between loving a child unconditionally and withholding love as a reward for optimum performance. It's a crucial difference in expectation levels: Is a child's happiness enough? Or must the parent be satisfied?

When I was eleven or twelve and swimming in regional meets, there was one girl, Stephanie, who had at least as much natural ability as I did. In fact, in a book I own that lists all the record times for all the events, year by year, broken down by age group, there she is—the record holder in practically every event but breaststroke. She was an unbelievable swimmer, the kind coaches always want on their team.

But it seemed to me she was never quite good enough for her father. Her dad was always there, at every meet, but he wasn't there to cheer. It seemed like he had a job to do, a mission to accomplish. Before the race he'd come over and chat with my parents to scope out the competition. "Is Summer racing well?" he'd ask them, or "How much does she practice?" During the race he'd stand alone on the pool deck, arms crossed, an unreadable, stony look on his face. Stephanie, who usually won, was equally emotionless—I never saw her raise her fist in victory, never heard her whoop or holler or make any sign that this sport was anything but *business* for her. She'd get out of the pool and it'd be like "Well, that's done, we can go home now."

Very matter-of-fact. When my mother had asked her, "Steph, you doing double workouts now?" she'd responded, "Yeah, *we're* going for the national age group records." I don't think *we* referred to her and her coach.

Ultimately, Stephanie was one of those swimmers I competed with who, despite proven talent, just faded away. She didn't go the distance.

I think she was missing the one thing that would take her all the way—to the Olympics and beyond. She was missing the passion, the sheer pleasure, that accounts for all true motivation, all true determination. And if she ever had the spark, I believe her parents blew on it so forcefully, they blew it out.

There are lots of parents that push their kids too hard. I run into them virtually every week. I've wanted to shake these parents, make them see what they were doing to their kid in the name of encouragement. *You're going about this all wrong!* I'd want to say. *You're going to kill any future she has in this sport!*

These are parents who would deny they are living through their child, manipulating an outcome for their own satisfaction. These are parents who don't trust their child to find an interest; they insist on providing one. These are parents who don't trust their child to have a passion strong enough to motivate self-improvement; they insist on substituting their own. These are parents who don't trust their child to learn by experience; they'd rather select the experience and dictate the lesson, because *they're the parent; they know best.* These are parents who've lost sight of what parenting is, which is supporting a child through the lessons taught by experience, until the child knows for himself or herself what's best.

These people are not monsters. They're simply blinded to what they're doing, blinded by what they consider to be selfless dedication to their child. "I only want the best for her," a father will say. "I can't let her throw away her talent," a mother will plead. "She'll thank me later," goes the thinking. "I'm only doing this for her own good." The pushiness comes from the best of intentions, if the worst of ambitions. These parents simply have a very distinct vision for their child, a particular outcome in mind that takes priority over all others. Sooner or later, silently or vocally, they communicate what that outcome is.

I'm not saying that parents shouldn't entertain high expectations for their child; I am saying that high expectations should remain undefined, open to possibilities only the child can imagine for herself. Too many parents these days have already filled in the blank. There's no room for the child to pencil in her own dreams. And that's the huge irony: the parents who push hardest in the most singular direction are doing the very thing that will deny them the outcome they want most.

The secret of my parents' success, I think, boils down almost to this: They had no binding expectations of me or my brother. My mom expected us to grow up into responsible adults, people who understood the importance of personal accountability, people who were decent and honest in their dealings with others. That outcome wasn't negotiable. Everything else was, however. She supported us in our passions and expected only that we would do our best. What that best was—how far and in what direction we went—that was up to us. "You can do whatever you set your mind to, Summer" was her constant reminder. When I set my mind to excelling at swimming, she was right there behind me. She knew all my times, she knew exactly whom I was competing against, she knew just what I needed in order to move up to the next level, just so she could better provide whatever I needed from her to continue in my journey. She never mapped that journey. She followed me.

Although I must admit my mother did have one burning ambition for me. She wanted me to be an accomplished horsewoman. She adored horses and riding, probably because she grew up in Nebraska, where there wasn't much else for a girl to do. It seemed perfectly logical to her that I would turn out to be just a fabulous equestrienne. So for six months, when I was about five, she trotted me over to the stables and paid for lessons, hoping I'd come to love being around horses, loping around the ring, and hanging out with all the other riders.

I didn't. The stable, as I remember it, was a frightening place, especially after this monster of a horse stepped on my foot. And I did not take to the saddle. We've got pictures of me on a pony, going around the ring, and I'm dead asleep. No sooner would I get situated and the horse would start that rhythmic trot than my head would start bobbing and I'd nod off.

My mother was disappointed. But as badly as she had wanted this one interest to take hold, as fond as she was of this vision of the two of us riding into the sunset, she wasn't about to force it on me.

"I thought it would be so special, having this mother-daughter thing, this sport we could share," she's told me since. "But it wasn't your thing. I had to accept it. I mean, as a parent, you've got to encourage your kids to try things, but there comes a point where you've got to ask yourself, 'How much is it for the child, and how much is it for the parent?'"

As for my dad's expectations of me—it wasn't in his nature to plot out my future potential. He was intent on enjoying me and Trev for who we were, during the hours we were with him. It was the potential of the moment he was interested in. "Who's up for the ten-o'clock movie?" he'd ask us at 9:45 P.M. "Wanna go? Think you can stay awake?" Or say he'd heard about a crawdad festival a hundred miles away. "Wanna go? Whaddya say?" It was almost a dare, these last-minute invitations: *Are you spontaneous enough?* His life ambition was to have fun, and it's fair to say that was the only ambition he pinned on us. *Life's a party! You're invited! Go out there and enjoy it!*

The only time my father entertained any expectations of others was in his marriage, and it got him into trouble. I know he had expectations of my mom and her role in their partnership. He was a traditionalist: If he worked hard all day making money, he expected to come home, put his feet up, click on the TV, and drink a beer while his wife fixed dinner. If Mom asked him to watch us kids for a half hour so she could run to the grocery store, he'd have said, "Not my job, Barbara—get a sitter." ("Yeah," he'll say to me now whenever I accuse him of some awful behavior toward Mom, "I probably did say something like that.") Raising kids, cleaning the house, fixing dinner—that was what he expected his wife to do. He didn't want her to work, not after we came along, even though he was under tremendous pressure, financially, with building a practice and building a new home. So he started resenting her for doing so "little," for seemingly not pulling her weight. When she got a part-time job coaching swimming, he thought she was skipping out on her duties at home. "Your mom's out swimming, and I'm layin' tile" was how he explained it to me once. He didn't appreciate her contribution, so she was angry. And he was angry with her for being angry all the time and not appreciative of what he was contributing.

I share all this because I think those expectations he had of my mom—and her rebellion against them, and his failure to understand her rebellion—led to the blowup of their marriage. If he learned anything from that, it was probably the wisdom of not forcing anybody you love into the box of your design. Divorce, too, made him appreciate us, as maybe he never had before when he was just the guy who brought home the bacon. Having to be both a mom and a dad to us for six months of the year involved him in our lives in a way he'd never known before. He got to be intensely grateful we were a part of his life. It never occurred to him to ask for more than that from us.

For years my father actually resented my swimming, because it seemed too competitive, too serious, too goal-oriented, and way, way too time-consuming. "Why does a swim meet have to take all day?" he'd ask me. "A soccer match lasted an hour!" "And swim practice—why does it have to be every afternoon, every Saturday, all year round, summers and vacations included?" He loved nothing better than to learn that my practice was canceled. If the phone rang before it was time for him to take me, he'd hover over it, listening while I picked up, waiting, praying for an excuse not to go. If it was the phone tree calling to say the pool was being cleaned, no practice today, he'd whoop and shout and dance. "How 'bout we go over to Scandia racetrack?" He'd wink. "Wanna go go-carting?"

My dad got involved in swimming, not as The Father of a Serious Athlete, but as Bob "Lemme buy you a beer" Sanders. He gave everybody else in my sport what he gave me: a chance to lighten up, an opportunity to take the stakes a little less seriously, a breather from the stranglehold of expectations. When we were in Rome in 1994 for the World Championships, almost a year after I'd retired from competitive swimming, my dad still felt obliged to loosen up the parents of the athletes, buy them drinks, tell them jokes, take their minds off the event, essentially, to *keep their expectations in check.* "We need him around all the time," total strangers kept telling me. Even Janet Evans's mom, who admits she lived and breathed her daughter's career, would quit talking about Janet and brighten when my dad arrived on the scene. When my club teammates and I started being referred to as the New Kids on the Block, my father organized the parents into a club of their own, the Old Farts Around the Corner, who convened two hours before every meet in a bar somewhere. Naturally, my dad was elected president. He and Tom Wagstaff, who was secretary, used to draw up formal notes of their meetings. The minutes would read like "Then Sanders went to the bar and bought a round of . . ." They'd send off these minutes to U.S. Swimming. To this day, everybody in U.S. Swimming knows my dad; he's infamous.

It's interesting that my dad was the one who downplayed the importance of athletic achievement, since he was a track-and-field star in high school. Every once in a while he'd bring up his track days and talk about them kind of wistfully. It was our theory that he never reached his potential. "Yeah, I coulda been pretty good at track," he'd agree, knocking down a beer in his La-Z-Boy. "I guess I probably should have worked at it." But he never felt or expressed the desire that Trevor and I make up for him. He loved that we were involved in sports—Trevor and I played a lot of them, not only soccer and swimming. He built a sport court in his backyard for us, along with the pool. He was and still is, in fact, a total sports fanatic: there isn't a professional league he doesn't track, year round. When I started making the Olympic cut—when he saw me darn near make the 1988 Olympic team, as a fifteen-year-old—he got tremendously excited and proud. Ask him what his greatest moment was, and he'll say Barcelona, summer of '92, watching me win my medals.

But expectations of Olympic greatness, back when I was reminding him to take me to practice? No way. My future was a blank slate for *me* to fill.

I've wondered if my parents' lack of pushiness and ambition for me came from the fact that they hadn't set their own sights sky-high. My father was ambitious only to the extent that it enabled him to have the money to live comfortably, relax, and have fun. My mother had grown up and married without ever really exploring her potential; she'd wanted to push herself, but found no one highly supportive of that drive, not her parents, not my dad. What if my parents had been superachievers themselves? Would they have been more inclined to push Trevor and me?

I'll never know. But I have talked to Olympic athletes who now have children of their own, children old enough to be competing in sports. I've asked my medal-winning buddies what expectations they have, if any. *Do you want your kids to be athletes? Do you want them to play your sport? Is it important they be good at it, even superior at it?*

"Are you kidding?" says Karch Kiraly, the three-time volleyball gold medalist, who has two boys, seven and eight. "Having them play volleyball competitively is the last thing on my mind.

I'm trying to expose them to every sport imaginable, but not on an organized level. Sports have gotten too organized and too serious at too young an age for too many kids. When I was growing up, a lot of the neighborhood kids played pickup sports; now we've got sign-ups. I didn't play in any tournament until I was eleven; now kids are pushed into organized play at the age of five. I think that can burn a kid out. Kids need time to be kids, to have fun."

Dan Jansen, the world-record-holding speed skater, finds it a little harder to have no athletic expectations of his daughter. "I'll be pitching a ball to her," he says, "or having her skate, and she'll get frustrated to the point of quitting. So I have to think, *How far do I want to make her try?* My pride says, 'I want her to be good at this.' But my instinct tells me, 'Let her be done when she wants to; she's only five, let her stop! She has so much time, just lie back!' "

What makes Dan stifle his pride, Karch protect his kids from pressure, and me so certain my own parents had the right idea not to push me is that all of us know in our heart of hearts that the reason we went to the very pinnacle of our chosen pursuit was the simple fact that we were free to do the choosing and the pursuing—at our own pace.

"I remember playing volleyball when I wanted to, because I wanted to," Karch asserts. "I'm still playing because I love it. I don't think I would have lasted this long if my father had pushed me. I'd have burned out years ago."

A LOT OF Olympians have shared their life story, either in book form or on the motivational-lecture circuit or in some network magazine segment. Look for common threads in those stories—reasons why these particular individuals took athletic ability and competitive drive and made themselves into champions—and a couple of things should pop out at you.

A lot of these star athletes, for instance, got very early starts. Bonnie Blair was on skates at two, Dan Jansen at four. I swam before I was out of diapers. Tara Lipinski was cutting figures at the age of six and a half. Every gymnast you can think of was practically born on a balance beam. It would seem we all got the gold eventually because we'd been at our sport longer than anybody else. We'd been given that precious jump start, that early exposure—and that's what a good parent would do if he or she wanted a star athlete: start 'em young.

But for every champion who was a child prodigy, I can show you another who discovered his Olympic sport late—in adolescence, or in college, even. Norm Bellingham, the gold-medal kayaker, didn't sit in a kayak until he was twelve, and he didn't get serious until he was fifteen. Justin Huish, who captured the gold in archery in 1996, didn't shoot an Olympic-style bow until 1989, when he was fourteen, working in his dad's archery shop. Crissy Ahmann, the swimmer who won silver and gold during the 1992 Olympics, took up the sport in college. Matt Biondi, the most decorated male Olympian, with eleven medals, favored basketball over pool sports until he was fifteen. Even the child prodigies—winners like Dot Richardson, who was, at thirteen, the youngest woman ever to play on a major-league women's fast-pitch softball team, or Bonnie Blair, who qualified her first time out for the Olympic team, when she was fifteen—will tell you they played every sport there was, indiscriminately. Bonnie was twelve before it occurred to her that she wanted to skate more than anything else she'd enjoyed, and she'd enjoyed them all, from competitive cycling and track to gymnastics and even cheerleading.

Then there's the fact that so many Olympic athletes had athletic parents. It stands to reason that Olympians are born, not raised: athleticism does run in families. My own dad was pretty good in track and field. Dot Richardson says her dad's track records still stand in a high school outside of Rochester, New York, and that her mom, who played fast-pitch softball as a teenager, could run even faster than her dad. Matt Biondi's dad was a career coach, although not of swimming.

But for every Olympian who comes from athletic stock, I can show you another who comes from parents who didn't even understand sports, let alone play them. Norm Bellingham's mom and dad are both academics, both graduates of the University of Chicago; his older brother won a Westinghouse scholarship to MIT. Debi Thomas, the world-champion figure skater who took a bronze in the 1988 Olympics, was raised by a mother who was an accomplished pianist with a degree in mathematics and an M.B.A. Karch Kiraly's dad is a physician with an additional master's in engineering; his mom has a master's in library science.

There's one other unmistakable trend among Olympians: a lot of them happen to be the youngest child. It's uncanny. Look at Dan Jansen and Bonnie Blair, speed skating's undisputed champions. He's the youngest of nine, she's the youngest of six. I'm the second of two, Matt Biondi's the third of three. The more you look, the more evident it becomes that there's something about being the baby of the family that makes for Olympic potential.

I think I know what it is, and it supports my own theory about what Olympians truly have in common: parents who never pushed. Bonnie Blair's a perfect example. Her parents were hands-off, in part because they had their hands full with her five siblings. When Bonnie was born, her dad was fifty-two, her mom was forty-five. "They were exhausted!" says Bonnie. "They were cooked!" Dan Jansen says the same thing: if his parents had ever entertained any particular ambitions for their offspring, by the time Dan arrived, they'd long since seen the folly of trying to impose them. "Not that my parents weren't concerned or involved," he says, "but they'd been through it eight other times."

The youngest tends to be competitive, too—a survival tactic, to hear Dan and Bonnie tell it. "We had to compete," says Bonnie, "just to be included. If we were going to stay with the family, then we were going to the rink. It never occurred to us that we couldn't keep up out there just because we were a lot younger."

But a competitive drive is not something that parents have anything to do with. Siblings, friends, peers, birth order, and inborn nature make a kid competitive, not a parent. It's the same with athletic ability; I'd say athletic talent is inborn. Yet it's pretty obvious that none of these things—being born the youngest, being born athletic, having a competitive drive, or being a child prodigy—guarantees Olympic glory or even champion-level performance. Otherwise, think how many high-school jocks would be playing their sport in the major leagues right now instead of watching them on TV. There has to be something else, and I'm betting it's something not inborn. You have to believe in your own potential, a belief that if you put your mind and soul to a task, and spare nothing in the giving of what you've got, anything is possible.

This is what parents can nurture. Parents do a lot of important things, fill a lot of critical needs, but when it comes to fostering achievement, it all comes down to helping their child come to feel confident and in complete control of her destiny. Parents who seize control of that destiny are in effect saying to the child, We don't think you've got what it takes to figure out what's best for you, or You can't be trusted with anything so important as your own future. It's the worst kind of undermining. It's the most painful vote of no confidence. It's the kind of unspoken parental input that even a gifted early-starting competitive youngest child could never overcome, could never triumph over.

Whereas parents who put their child in the driver's seat—even when, or especially when, the stakes are very high—these parents are sending a hugely empowering message: You can do it. You don't need anybody, or anything, to bring you success. It's all up to you—and you have all the time in the world, so enjoy it.

Bonnie Blair tells a story that shows what this kind of parenting looks like better than I can describe it. When she was twelve, her dad drove her three and a half hours away to a competition in Chicago, a meet that required an overnight stay in a hotel. Bonnie skated the first day, but on the second, the temperature dropped until the windchill factor was about eighty degrees below zero. The rink was right off Lake Michigan. "We're talkin', *it was cold*," says Bonnie.

Minutes before she was to compete, she told her dad she didn't want to skate. "It's just too cold," Bonnie said to him. "I want to stay in the van."

He let her. No punishing stare, no mean body language, no biting comment about the time and the money he'd put into the trip.

"He was always a man of few words," she explains, "but he didn't give me a hard time at all. I watched him from the van, out there in the freezing cold, while he timed the other skaters. When he was done timing, he got back in the van and we drove home.

"Here we've driven all this way," she emphasizes, "and spent money on dinner and a hotel, money he really didn't have. I tell him I don't feel like skating, and he says, 'Fine!' If that doesn't tell you how not-pushy he was, I don't know what would."

YOU CAN LOOK for all sorts of patterns in Olympic athletes, come up with all sorts of formulations for success, but the only one that remains utterly consistent is this one about parenting style. Every champion athlete, every Olympic gold medalist has the same story: They were in charge of their own dream. If their destination had been mapped out, they couldn't have maintained their interest in the journey. And if they'd been pushed, the fire that drove them would have been snuffed out.

"My dad didn't drive to exceed in sports through me," explains champion swimmer Matt Biondi, "because he'd been around sports enough to understand they're not for parents to brag about their child. They're about the process, about learning to improve. They're about doing what you do best. Consistently. And honestly."

On that point, he speaks for us all.

2

Blowing on the Spark:
All About Motivation

Where does that spark first come from? Do we love what we're good at? Or are we good at what we love doing?

It doesn't matter, so long as love is part of it. It's the emotion that can make the difference between a good athlete and a great one, a dogged worker and an inspired one, even a silver medalist and a gold medalist. Training is never enough, says figure skater Debi Thomas: "Look at Michelle Kwan and Tara Lipinski at the Nagano Games: Tara won because she had an emotional component kick in. She had a ball, and she skated the program of her life!"

The Emotional Component: A Passion

A desire to play or perform that is there no matter what the obstacles, no matter what the outcome—Debi Thomas had it. She didn't like training, but going into competition, having it

all come together, and getting an audience to stand on its feet—
"I can't explain what a fantastic feeling that was," she says. "I
was always a very real skater, not one of these people who can
practice smiling. When I was on, you could see it. You could
feel it."

Dot Richardson says she used to feel selfish playing softball,
because she loved it so much. "The feeling of the ball ripping
off the bat," she explains, "the feeling of the ball coming into
the glove, that moment it's yours, and then seeing the sweat fly
off your arm as you throw it, seeing the seams of the ball—
there's no greater feeling in the world than that, where you're so
focused on what you're doing. I love that feeling.

"Now," says Dot, who coaches her own fast-pitch teams, "I
ask my girls why they play: Is it for that feeling, for the love of
it? Or for getting a scholarship or pleasing their parents or
winning a medal? I know who will make it, who will reach her
dreams and goals. To want to *live* the dream is different from
wanting to have it. That motivation comes from within. A
coach, a parent can't force it."

A parent can't force it. A parent can't bribe it. A parent can't
argue its importance. You can't force a kid to stick out a sport
by insisting he's going to get a lot out of it, any more than you
can convince him to eat brussels sprouts by pointing out they're
nutritious.

But a parent *can* exert a ton of influence by *showing* a child
that being passionately involved—in a sport, in a play, in an
orchestra, in photography, in whatever—is something enjoyable
and rewarding. Parents need passionate interests of their own,
things they do because they love the sheer doing of them. If you
swim for your own pleasure or you show how much you enjoy

watching or coaching swimming or, at the very least, you take pleasure in swimming by watching it as an avid fan—a child who sees that kind of passion is going to want some for herself. It's infectious. Parents who want their children to pick up something and work at it can inspire that behavior best by modeling it.

My dad, as I've mentioned, is passionate about sports—all sports. My dad is passionate about having fun, too. He put the pool and the sport court in our backyard, and he took just as much pleasure playing in them as we did. My mom loved to swim, too. Had there been intramural opportunities for girls when she was growing up, I'm sure she would have been on the swim team. As it was, they signed my brother up for the Roseville summer rec league (I can just hear my mother saying, "It's good to have a child's energies in something productive—too many kids have too much time on their hands"), and that's all it took to get me interested in competitive swimming.

Whatever Trevor was doing, I had to get in on it. He was my older brother, so anything he did was automatically cool. Throughout our childhood, he had this power over me, this way of making whatever he was interested in seem way cooler than whatever I was interested in. I would do anything just to be included in his circle. If his friends were over, playing Wiffle ball, I'd agree to be the catcher for the entire game, even though it was the position no one else wanted. The ball would foul off in funny directions, my knees would get tired, I'd get hit with the bat. But I did it, because otherwise, I wouldn't get to play at all. I wasn't allowed to hit. "Can't I have just one turn at bat?" I'd plead. "Just one?" Trevor might let me have one turn—three swings, that was it. "But I didn't even hit it! One more chance!"

Blowing on the Spark

I'd cry. Nope. I was the catcher and Trevor was the star hitter. It was that way with everything.

So when Trevor joined the swim team at the age of six, I told my mom that's what I wanted to do, too. I could've hated water, could have gone into allergic shock over chlorine, and still, if Trevor and his friends were going to spend their summer swimming, I'd find a way to be in the lane next to him. I was only four, but I could make my way across a pool width. Trevor thought I was too young, too tiny, too incompetent to be on a swim team, so that cinched it. More than anything, I wanted to prove him wrong. *See? I CAN SO BE WITH YOUR FRIENDS!*

Proving someone wrong was a major motivating force with me. It's how I learned to swim. We had our own pool, which was pretty typical in my town. My parents hired a swim instructor to come to our house and teach us before we had a chance to fall in and drown. I wasn't yet two years old at the time. I used to cry just at the sight of this guy, just at the sound of his name (Mark—pretty funny, considering I married a Mark), and I'd keep crying during our lesson. I took my first swim test when I was three. According to my mother, my instructor tried to take me out of the pool before I'd made my way across. But I wouldn't let him, even though I was sputtering and flailing something awful. "I DO IT! I DO IT!" I insisted. And I did it, either to get away from him or to prove I didn't need him anymore. I was a determined kid, right from the beginning. Even a mere suggestion that I couldn't pull off something— especially something that Trevor was doing—and my response was "Oh, yeah? Just watch me."

My parents should have made better use of Trevor—he was so influential. Anything he took even slightly seriously, I took up with a vengeance. On the other hand, even a laugh or snigger from him had the power to stop me in my tracks. The summer I was eight, my mom enrolled me in a children's acting workshop. She thought it might be fun, something to do in the summertime, something to get me to be a little less shy. She didn't sign up Trevor. I was scared to death. *Am I going to be left here?* I wondered that whole first day. Our first workshop, we were supposed to do a pantomime of Dorothy and Toto, skipping and picking flowers—each one of us was to take a turn at it. This one boy got up there, and he was *awesome.* He was a more convincing Dorothy than Judy Garland was. I prayed we'd run out of time before it was my turn. When I got up there I felt so self-conscious, so stupid, I could imagine Trevor laughing his head off at me. That killed it.

Trevor and I did take tennis lessons together. I wasn't all that bad. Maybe, if we'd had a tennis court in our backyard instead of a pool, or if my parents had played, I would've been more attracted to it and turned out to be a decent player. But Trevor, my idol, couldn't take the game seriously enough to play by the rules: "Hey, Summer: Let's see who can hit the balls the farthest OVER THE FENCE!" I could never resist a competition he started, so then we had to go collect all those balls outside the court. I got very tired of picking up balls. It seemed like that was all we did: Hit the net, pick up the balls. Serve badly, pick up the balls. Wait your turn . . . pick up the balls. It wasn't like swimming, where you'd just dive into the pool and go all out, with nothing to stop you, nothing to slow you down or hold you back. I couldn't get myself worked up enough on that court to really pay attention. I used to show up for my tennis lesson in flip-flops, which may give you some idea of my focus and dedication.

Trevor had the power, certainly, to influence my interests. But if I took up competitive swimming because of him, I chose to stick with it for a whole bunch of other reasons.

One really key reason was that my mom was there. She didn't drop us off at the Roseville pool and run to the store while we practiced. The fact that both her kids were going to be spending a good part of the summer swimming prompted her to volunteer as a coach's assistant. She helped out with the little kids, of which I was the youngest. She could have shown up with a lawn chair to watch us practice, or just come to watch meets, but the fact was, she enjoyed being with us, she enjoyed being with the other children, and she enjoyed the sport. That she got right in there, helping out, smiling and laughing, getting to know everybody, made it all the more fun for Trevor and me. I loved having her there.

I often think back to what her presence meant at my first meet. I was a splinter of a girl, shy by nature, not inclined to get up in front of a crowd of people and perform. The thought filled me with nervous terror, just as it had when I stood up in front of that stupid drama class. I managed to get up on the block, shivering with cold and fear. But when the starter asked if everyone was ready, my lower lip started to tremble, tears started welling up and spilling over, and little choking sounds came out of my mouth. A *lot* of people were watching—the whole town of Roseville, it seemed.

Suddenly, there was my mom. She'd been comforting all us little girls, but when she saw me, she held her hand up to the starter and came over. "It's just like practice," she said to me calmly. "Swim to Mary [my baby-sitter] and Dad. See? They're waving at you!" Then, because I was still crying, she said, "Summer, honey, you don't *have* to do this."

I stopped crying. My mother will tell you I got what would become my trademark look of Get-Out-of-My-Way determination, and then, at the whistle, dove off that block and swam as though sharks were lunging at my toes. And when I got out of the pool, having shaved maybe ten seconds off my usual time, I was grinning like my face was going to split. "You were strutting and swaying over to the coach to give him five," my mom recalls.

What a revelation! I could place, even win, just by trying hard! When everybody was proud of me—when I'd even amazed myself—it felt so good I couldn't wait to try even harder next time.

That's the whole secret of motivation. A little effort brings a little reward. A little reward sows a little confidence. A little confidence prompts a little more effort, an eagerness to take on a slightly greater challenge. Personal satisfaction brings confidence, and confidence inspires effort, until what started as a mere spark of interest has grown into a burning desire that can't be contained. The parent's role is limited but crucial: My mom being there gave me just the sense of security I needed to tap my own drive. She made it her job to keep things not too overwhelming, not too pressured, not too daunting. She made it her job to keep it fun. She made it her job to keep the fright out of failure. That allowed me to discover all sorts of motivations, all sorts of good reasons to keep swimming.

Sounds easy, doesn't it? But apparently it's not, because I get letters all the time from parents who are desperate to learn how to get their son or daughter motivated. They don't buy this idea of standing by enthusiastically. They're not willing to wait for motivation to build up on its own, so when their child seems "not to want it badly enough" they start to panic, start to believe drastic steps must be taken to jump-start their kid's race for excellence.

Could you just write a letter to my daughter? She'd be a terrific swimmer, if only she'd apply herself. But she won't. I'm thinking of changing her coach. . . .

Could you talk to my son? He's playing basketball, and I know he could be a great forward—he's got the height, he's got the coordination. It's just that he's not giving it his all. He doesn't want it badly enough, I guess. I thought you could be an inspiration. . . .

My daughter wants to quit swimming, but she'd be throwing away so much talent, so much training, so many years of hard work, I'm afraid to let her. What can I do to get her motivated again?

Once again, however, these parents are not monsters. They've simply gotten the wrong idea about how a child goes from a neighborhood sandlot to the major leagues. Their view of greatness—what it takes, where it comes from, how it flowers—is all backward. And I know how it happens to get that way.

Think about our notions of achievement, and you'll see they come from being shown only the end product, never the work-in-progress. We're all accustomed to seeing Olympians, for example, through the camera's lens. That lens focuses, though, on athletes performing only at the peak of their powers, at the culmination of their careers. The camera isn't interested in practice, where plenty of time is spent goofing off and screwing up; the camera doesn't bother to record Greg Louganis belly flopping into the water, or Nadia Comanici falling off the balance beam into the foam pit, or Magic Johnson sending an easy layup shot into the bleachers. We never see any of these achievers as kids, playing pranks on each other in the locker room. The camera doesn't go to any of their pizza parties, doesn't accompany the team on any trips out of town.

We're never shown anybody *having fun at the sport.*

By the time the camera invites us all in to watch, these guys are at the final stage, when practice looks like an ordeal, when everybody's focused and serious, when it seems like only super-human dedication and sacrifice and the promise of a medal could possibly account for the athlete being there at all.

If people know me, for example, it's as the nineteen-year-old swimmer who won a couple of medals during the Barcelona Games. That makes me unrecognizable as a swimmer who, like most kids swimming right now, sometimes whined about going to practice, sometimes quit swimming altogether. Parents have only the image of Summer Sanders that the camera has shown them, the super swimmer, the one who must have never flinched from an early-morning workout, the one who willingly got up at 4 A.M. to swim 6,000 yards twice a day, six days a week. And they can only conclude, from this image of me, that I must have been one weird child, because who in their right mind would *love* all that sheer drudgery? That's what they conclude when they get wind of my training over the years: the sheer sacrifice of it all, the weight of all those workouts added up. They can't see the fun, which is what propelled me all along. They're thinking, *jeez, THAT'S motivation—and if that's what it takes, then my kid sure doesn't have it. I've got to light a fire under him NOW.*

Looking at motivation from the wrong end of the telescope, from the Olympic end backward, instead of from a backyard pool forward, makes you blind to the most basic truth: kids will try something new as long as they feel safe and loved, and they'll stick to it if they can see some fun or reward in it—friends, candy, pizza, road trips, and shiny trophies, for example. (A big part of my interest in going to the pool when I was little was the fact that my friends and I could pig out on boxes of Jell-O, which we smuggled from home and ate by licking our fingers and dabbing at the colored sugar right out of the box.) Anything that takes work down the road has got to be fun right from the start. It must involve friends, or the opportunity to make new ones. And there must be some reward for effort, some sense of progress, so that it's never pointless to try harder. Personal satisfaction, however small, should always be within reach.

Now, it can take a while for that initial spark of interest to build into a fire. Sometimes—a lot of the time—it just seems to smolder. But a parent who blows on it to speed things up is liable to blow it out altogether.

*   *   *

My mom, as I said, exerted a huge influence on me just by being there, at the pool, in a meaningful way: she was my security blanket at the very beginning, and then she was, by her example of dedication, an inspiration. Little kids don't say to themselves, *Gee, if it's worth Mom's time to be here doing this, then it's worth mine,* but on a subconscious level, that's what they understand. It gets back to what I said about parents modeling motivation, modeling involvement. Children follow in any footsteps that they can see lead to enjoyment.

I'll give you some more examples.

Karch Kiraly's dad played volleyball on weekends. It was his only break from a grueling schedule as a doctor on call who also moonlighted as a translator of scientific papers. He wouldn't see much of Karch during the week, so on Saturday mornings he'd get his only son out of bed and bring him to the club tournaments he played in. Karch's dad lived for these games. He'd get up at 3:30 A.M. in the dead of winter to drive through snow across the state of Michigan to play, and his son liked to come with him, if only to be with him.

"Even though I didn't play on the court," says Karch, who was seven when this started, "I have warm memories of all those Saturdays, with my dad and his teammates. While they were playing I'd watch, and I could see it wasn't just a competition; I could see the whole team chemistry, the male bonding, the social thing. I'd play pepper with my dad, or if he was busy, I'd shoot baskets in the gym by setting and bumping a volleyball, which made me a better player. But mostly, it was an opportunity to spend time with my dad. He was doing his three-year residency then, and, working so hard, sometimes the weekend was the only time I saw him."

Karch and his dad became teammates when Karch was ten. They played in a novice tournament on the beach in Corona del Mar, California; in beach volleyball, there are only two men on a side. "We had such a blast," he recalls. "Over the next four years, we played together exclusively, in novice tournaments, B-player, A-player, Double-A, and Triple-A games. We never won a tournament, but I really enjoyed those opportunities, playing with my dad, competing so well."

All the motivation Karch ever needed arose from the simple fact that playing this sport allowed him to be with his dad, sharing in what gave his dad great pleasure. Competition only intensified the feeling that they were a team, that with his dad by his side he was practically invincible. I can't imagine a better way to foster a healthy love of competition.

Dot Richardson has a similar story. She knew as a five-year-old that God had given her a gift for sports. She loved them all, throughout childhood and adolescence; if it wasn't softball, it was tetherball, soccer, ringers, tennis. But it was her dad who made her choice seem inevitable: He played catch with her. He couldn't coach her, as he did her brothers in Little League, because she was a girl, and back then girls didn't play baseball in any organized way. But that didn't stop him from indulging Dot's desire to play. Dot remembers the day they were hurling a ball back and forth and she chipped her front tooth. "He put his arm around me, we went inside, Mom freaked out—and yet, I felt so great! This happened because I got to play catch with my dad!"

That Dot's God-given ability was responsible for her phe-nomenal career as a fast-pitch softball player (she made the majors at the age of thirteen) is undisputed. But her passion for the game sparked and flared from those casual games of catch with her dad. All her life she would associate playing ball with the embrace of her father—with the happiest moments of her childhood.

Dan Jansen and Bonnie Blair started skating at the age of two, just because the rink was where Mom was, or Dad, or at least one of their siblings. Skating was just something their families did for fun. There was never any competitive pressure: if Bonnie fell asleep for her daily nap when her four-year-old peers were about to race, her mother let her. ("There will always be another one," she told anybody who raised an eyebrow at the sleeping competitor.) Throughout grade school, and junior high, both Bonnie and Dan were all-around athletes. She swam, she did gymnastics, she ran track, she cycled competitively, she even tried cheerleading. Dan's coaches thought he had the build and the speed to become a football star; they tried to get him to drop out of skating, because at the time it seemed like skating would get you nowhere, whereas football players had a future. But both Dan and Bonnie ultimately came back to skating. As Bonnie puts it, "It just came to me gradually that this was what I enjoyed the most. I never had any inclination to stop."

Oh, to be sure, lots of factors other than family influenced Dan and Bonnie to keep skating. Dan remembers how inspired he was by Eric Heiden, the gold medalist who trained in the same rink where Dan skated with his family; when Eric became a national hero, suddenly Dan felt that future was open to him, too. Bonnie remembers what a rush it was to qualify for the

Olympic trials her very first time out, at the age of fifteen. "Everything started to click for me then," she says. "I could see my own potential." But think about it: When all the people you love and look up to most in the world—your parents, your brothers, your sisters—are out there on the ice with you, from as early as you can remember, then wouldn't skating be the sport you felt most secure and comfortable and happy in? Wouldn't that comfort and joy make you feel you could afford to put more on the line, be more willing to risk failure? And isn't that what it takes to punch through to the next level, and the next, until before you even know it, you're darn near the top of the competitive pyramid?

THAT'S WHAT A parent, or a sibling, or a whole family can give: not motivation, but the seedbed for motivation to grow in. At an age when I still needed that extra assurance, that security blanket of a parent right by my side, my mother was there, right next to the racing block. Then, as I got to be older and more secure, she set an example. While we were in grade school, she'd get up at 5:30 A.M., drive over to the Sierra College pool, swim laps for an hour while we slept, and then have pancakes and eggs ready for us when we woke up. Later still, when I had 5:15 morning practices and we had to drive over to Sacramento, she and some of the other moms took advantage of the open lanes and eventually formed a little league of their own. We weren't swimming together, we weren't competing against each other, and once practice started, I hardly saw her, but swimming was this thing we shared, the source of our companionship.

We had our little ritual each morning. I always organized all my stuff the night before so that I could literally roll out of bed at 4:14, wake up my mom, put milk on my Grape-Nuts, pull on my clothes, wolf down my cereal, and get into the car by 4:25 A.M. We'd get to Sacramento by 5 A.M., and then it was a race to get into the pool. In California almost all the pools are outside, and at that hour, it'd be black as night and freezing cold. We kids wouldn't waste time out on the deck; we'd race from the locker room to dive into that steaming water.

We would, but not my mom. I'd have swum four laps and she'd still be sitting on the edge, stuffing her hair deep into her cap, adjusting these huge bug-eyed goggles on her face.

"Mom!" I'd say, exasperated. "Jump in!"

"I'm *getting* in, Summer. I have to ease my way in, that's all."

It was excruciating, watching her lower her body like she was doing a bar dip, all that strain and effort. Then she'd push off gently, so as not to splash her face, and she'd swim the first two laps with her head up. She looked ridiculous, doing the crawl like that.

I'd try and splash her, or if I was swimming in the next lane, I'd reach over and pinch her. "Put your head in!" I'd yell.

And she'd yell back, "It's just *too* cold!"

Every morning we went through this. But it was our thing. And it made us both appreciate each other's job: what it took, on her part, to be with me, to make my swimming possible; and what it took on my part to succeed as a swimmer.

"Every parent should have to make the effort to learn the strokes," my mom is fond of telling people. "I mean, to stand on the pool deck and criticize your child for not making junior national times—I want to say to these parents, 'Do you have any idea how difficult it is to swim that race? How many laps of butterfly can *you* do?' "

I'm not insisting that parents inspire dedication only by taking up the sport themselves. But as I look back on it, my mom's companionship and the pleasure she took in this—in coming with me, in getting in the pool, in putting up with my teasing—had a lot to do with my own commitment. I wanted to come to practice and work hard because I fed off personal satisfaction, but I also loved making my mom proud and happy, and since she knew so much about my sport, she could appreciate all that went into my winning. Winning was one of the few ways I could give back to the person I loved most. I didn't swim for my mom, and I didn't win for my mom, but I couldn't help but want her to feel rewarded. In that sense, she very clearly motivated me.

Still, I feel I have to emphasize, she didn't come out to "light a fire" under me. "Making me into a champion" was not what motivated her. Her own love for what she was doing motivated her. She enjoyed swimming, enjoyed being with me, enjoyed the pleasure I took from my sport. And because she loved being a part of my sport, I loved being a part of it even more.

HAVING A PARENT around who's clearly enjoying herself is probably critical for little kids. I'd be the first to admit, however, that by grade school most kids aren't going out for a sport because Mom or Dad might be there. They love their parents, they need their parents, but it's their friends they want to hang out with.

I was no exception. From the age of six, I swam year-round

with our local club, SIAC (SIerra Aquatic Club, which ultimately merged into CCA, California Capital Aquatics), because it gave me a whole set of friends and experiences outside of school. I felt like I had twice as much fun, and did twice as many cool things as anybody who just went home and watched TV every afternoon.

Club swimming was more about having friends and having a great time with them than about competing or winning races. I have a picture of me that pretty much captures my early motivation: I'm maybe six—my front teeth are missing—and my friend Megan and I are sitting on the concrete pool deck playing patty-cake. My hair is all tangled and wrecked-looking because I wouldn't wear a swim cap. We're at a meet in Sacramento, and because it was so cold that day it actually started snowing, we're bundled up in our sleeping bags and parkas. I remember our moms were absolutely miserable. I remember they came over to us and said, "Hey! You know, we don't have to stay! It's so cold, why don't we go get pizza? Or go see a movie?" They were dying to leave. But we wouldn't let them. "We wanna STAY!" we shouted. Megan and I were having way too much fun.

With my teammates—whether it was a summer recreation league, club swimming, or the high-school team—there was never a question of "fitting in" or wondering if I "belonged," because we all had this great common element: our sport. Being part of a team was a very empowering, very secure thing. I felt like I was part of something important, something special. We got to do things most other kids, it seemed, got left out of. We'd go out of town, stay in motels, live out of our duffel bags, never change out of our swimsuits, eat breakfast in restaurants, go out on the town and explore, stay in and play endless card games.

All we had to do in exchange for these privileges was swim. A win-win deal, we thought.

Taking ourselves or our performance too seriously was out of the question, even during big away meets like the Far Westerns (to which any club was invited) or the Junior Nationals. Each morning of the meet we'd wake up, find out which events we were supposed to participate in, scrawl our event numbers on our hands so we'd know when to show up on the blocks, and then concentrate on the *really* key issues: whose parents had a camper or a tent we could hang out in, whether we wanted to play Uno, or Spit, or Speed, whether or not we could get away with a massive shaving-cream war in the hotel hallways, who had the best supply of snack foods ("Did you bring grapes? Is there any celery and peanut butter in your camper?"), when we were going to go out to a movie, and how we were going to get back at the boys for the last prank. (One time my brother molded PowerBars into what looked like turds, and left them on the starting blocks at the pool.) Not until I was in college did meets become serious enough for us to opt out of the midnight movie, or take a pass on the sausage at breakfast, or go lie on our beds instead of playing Hearts so we could concentrate on the race to come.

I swam because it was my ticket to what felt like an endless play date, or a family vacation. Just anticipating going away for a swim meet was enough to get me excited for four or five weeks, and that excitement spilled over into my workouts. It was exactly like getting ready to go away on vacation. "Does everybody know where they're staying?" my coach would ask each practice, or "Does everybody have their ride worked out?" We'd think what to pack, what snacks to bring, whom we were likely to run into, what kind of fun we could expect to have. We'd wonder what the pool would be like, what kind of facility it'd be. We'd imagine the town, we'd imagine its restaurants and malls, and we'd form a picture of the hotel we were going to inhabit for anywhere from three to eight days.

For my first Junior Nationals, in Grand Forks, North Dakota, my coach got us lodgings at some place called The Ambassador. We had all sorts of expectations about how fancy it was going to be, with bellboys and a lobby and probably its own restaurant. Well, we pulled up in a snowstorm to this one-story row of sixteen rooms, all so tiny we had to rent the entire motel. The Ambassador was like any motel, in that you drove up practically to your doorknob, but there was a glass hallway in front of all the doors. The first night we were there, I had one of my nerve-induced sleepwalking attacks. I got up on the bed, opened the door, banged on the glass wall, and screamed, "It's SNOWING! Everybody, wake up, we're going to be late for the meet! We've GOT TO GO, NOW!" Everybody did wake up, and they were not excited. For the rest of our weeklong stay, they put furniture in front of my door at night so that I wouldn't be able to walk out and do it again.

If it wasn't the hotel, it was the trip itself that made for you-had-to-be-there stories we'd be telling and retelling. For one meet in Clovis, California, my mom and another swimmer, Terry, and her mom shared the three-and-a-half-hour drive from Roseville together. Terry was sixteen; I was only twelve. I watched her every move, fascinated to be this close for this long to one of the *big kids*, especially now that I was included in their meets. And Terry was fascinating: Practically everything her mother did, she took issue with it. "GOD, Mom, how can you wear *those shoes* with *those pants?*" Terry would say, or "Why is your hair like that?" or "Can't you pick a *good* radio station?" Terry would drive for a while, and if her mom suggested she use her blinker, Terry would be all over her. "You know, I don't need my turn signal for *every* turn! People will *know* I'm turning!" Then there was the way Terry ate: She would not let a vegetable pass her lips. We pulled into some truck stop, and everything she wanted to order, she had to ask the waitress to check for vegetables. "It's minestrone with *vegetables?* Can you, like, *pick out* the vegetables?" (All Terry lived on was chips and chocolate and junk, and she was a *rail.*) Getting to spend time with Terry was like having a big sister (which I didn't have) show you all the ropes of adolescence. I felt clued in after that car ride. My mom and I still remember and laugh about it.

Major away meets like Far Westerns really felt like a family vacation, because both my parents would be there, despite the divorce, along with Trevor, who had no choice but to come and watch. We'd stay in some motel, in two rooms, or maybe my mom would stay with friends and Trevor and I had to share a bed. I was famous for sleeptalking and sleepwalking, especially during meets when my nerves were strung tight. One night I did the breaststroke, right there in bed, asleep. Another time I rolled over and hit Trevor, so he hit me back. "WHAT THE HELL!" I screamed, "Dad, Trevor's HITTING me!" My father yelled at Trevor to stop. "I am NOT sleeping in the same bed as you anymore," Trevor hissed back at me. But then the next day, there he'd be, cheering me on, helping the coaches time, being my biggest fan.

If I wasn't hanging out with my family on these trips, I was seeing friends I hadn't seen since the last meet. One girl, Darcy, was my best out-of-town swim friend—and also archrival. Maybe because we shared so much—the same events, similar times, the same competitive drive—we sought each other out when we weren't in the pool. Our parents got to know each other, and Darcy became just one more reason to get really psyched about going out of town for a few days to swim my guts out. Her parents had a camper, and we'd sit at that cramped fold-out dinette, talking about boys, eating Doritos or celery and peanut butter (my absolute favorite), playing cards. I can remember going over to her house, too, when Far Westerns were held in her hometown, and marveling at her collection of stuffed animals and all her video games. I remember her hair: it was so completely destroyed by chlorine, you could break it just by bending it. And of course, I remember her race: the 100 IM. She was *so* tough.

I swam for the privilege of these trips and the fun I had with my friends. But my parents still played a critical role, and not just because I didn't yet have a driver's license. My dad, for instance, could get me to calm down just by joining me for breakfast. I can remember coming off the cafeteria line with a tray full of pancakes and sausage and sitting down with my dad, who had just made his rounds socializing with all the other parents he knew (which was practically every parent in the room). He'd sit back, sip his coffee, and read his sports page like there was just all the time in the world for relaxing and eating. There wasn't: I was about to go into the pool, and loading myself down with sausage links was a terrible idea. But it didn't matter back then. What counted was that my dad was happy to be there—with me, with his coffee and paper, and with his circle of friends. Whether I won or lost out there in the next couple hours, he'd still find the same pleasure in these breakfasts and my company. I swam better knowing that. Back then, it didn't matter what I ate, it mattered that I had this reassuring, calming moment with my dad.

His attitude helped me overcome all sorts of hurdles—like once, the most awful ear infection. It was my second Far Western, and I was miserable over my ear—not because it hurt so much but because I had to have cotton in there and pull my cap down over it so that I looked like what I thought was a total dork. We had our big breakfast ritual, though, and I forgot about my ear, or at least stopped thinking it was such a big deal. I went out and won my first event, the 50-meter freestyle. I was beyond excited. I got a T-shirt with purple writing and a purple aqua bear (the mascot of our sponsor), and I got the first of so many Far Western plaques that I covered my whole bedroom wall with them at my dad's house.

THE THOUGHT OF all those plaques brings me to the third and most sustaining source of motivation: personal satisfaction. It didn't take any medal, any trophy, any public recognition for me to feel satisfied with myself in my sport. I could take great satisfaction just in finishing a really hard workout. Practice was hard enough to be totally absorbing; I literally could think of nothing but getting my body through the water as efficiently as possible. A bad grade, an embarrassing moment, a falling-out with somebody—I had to put any and all distractions aside simply to get through practice. By the time I'd spent every last ounce of energy and will on my swimming, I found that those worries had either washed clean away or been put in their proper perspective. Nothing could get me down for long provided I could feel I had mastered the challenge my coach set before me every day. Practice gave me that supreme satisfaction of having accepted a very tough piece of work and gotten it *done*.

I know that swimming from one end of the pool to the other has a sameness to it that makes people marvel how anybody could do it day after day. But the sameness, to those of us training, provided a convenient measure of our progress. The lanes never changed, but we did: the harder we worked, the faster we swam. The clock never lied. And that daily proof that I was improving, progressing—it filled me with satisfaction and emptied me of any anxiety. Every single day. That's how I found the energy and willingness to do it day after day, six mornings a week, five afternoons a week, eleven months of the year. That's how I stayed motivated.

If truth be told, I could be motivated to swim all-out record-breaking sets during practice just by imagining that some boy I wanted to notice me happened to be in the stands, watching me kick ass. One guy in particular, Scott, didn't even go to my high school (he swam on a different Sacramento team), but I had it in my head that Scott just *might* be up there in the bleachers, just *might* happen by when I was doing my workout, just *might* happen to catch me at my all-time peak performance. Naturally, I was too shy to ever approach him and actually *speak*, but thinking about him and how impressed he'd be if he saw me kickin' butt got me halfway through high school. I'd literally say to myself at the beginning of practice, "I have to do well, I gotta get out and be tough"—role playing, because it'd take my mind off how much pain I was in for after this really grueling set. I never knew if he saw me, but imagining he did would be enough to make me feel great, so pleased at having this opportunity to show him what I could do, how special I was.

Scott wasn't the only guy I swam harder to please. My coach, Mike Hastings, inspired me precisely because he *did* notice my extra effort. Having him be proud of me, having him race up and down the pool deck with excitement over my performance—well, there just wasn't a better feeling in the world. Likewise with my mom and my dad: no matter how old I get, hearing one of them say, as I've heard them say all my life, "I'm so *proud* of you" only makes me want to make them prouder.

But nobody—not a supportive parent, not a stellar coach, not a boy, not a best friend—could *make* me do anything I didn't already want to do for myself.

Had my parents set goals for me like "*You're* going to the Junior Nationals," or "You could hold the age-group record in the breaststroke," I would have been robbed of all the simple satisfactions—shaving a second off my 100-meter backstroke time, for instance, or finishing a hard practice set that I didn't think I could do, or getting my coach to jump up and down with excitement over my emerging butterfly technique. But they didn't set goals for me or define what was "progress," so the smallest indication that I was making headway thrilled me to no end. It was all up to me what I wanted to achieve. I wrote down my goal times and pasted them on my bathroom mirror. They were for me to know, for me to decide what it would take to meet them. It was for me and me *only* to determine what was rewarding and what wasn't. This independence was a hugely motivating, empowering gift my parents gave me.

Parents I meet these days don't even see how they deny their child this power. I've heard parents say, "Oh, she's too young to compete!" as if to protect their child from failing at a goal she's not ready to reach for. I know their intentions are good—no one likes to see their child be defeated—but I think it's not up to the parent to define the boundaries. Even a three-year-old has some grasp of her capabilities. I did; I knew I could swim that pool width, and I wasn't about to let my swim teacher tell me otherwise. Likewise, when I was four, I could have decided to step down and not swim that first race—my mother reminded me I had the option—but I didn't. Children know what they're ready to try.

Where a parent can make all the difference, I think, is in helping a child define failure, not success. A child who tries something that's beyond her capabilities doesn't need a parent stepping in to redefine "appropriate" goals—that only under-scores her sense of failure. Instead, the parent should help her child see that not meeting a goal isn't any reflection on her self-worth. Failure is not something to be ashamed of; it means you tried something a little beyond your reach. It means you've just learned a little bit more to help you get a little closer to realizing that goal the next go-round. If a parent can help a child see that failure carries no penalty, then it shouldn't matter what goals the child sets for herself. Her best might not be good enough to win at first, but that doesn't mean it's failure.

I can remember, during the '92 Olympics, coming out of the pavilion right after I'd failed to win the 100-meter butterfly, which was the longest of long shots for me, but which the media had hyped everyone into believing might be my second of five medal performances. Parents and friends weren't allowed near us as we boarded the bus for the Olympic Village, but there was my mom, waiting for me on the other side of the eight-foot chain-link fence that separated us.

"Mom," I cried out to her, my voice cracking, "did I really do that bad?"

"Honey, that was a *great* swim," she yelled back through the fence. "The hundred-meter 'fly's not even your best event, and you got your lifetime second-best time! There was *nothing wrong* with your swim!"

A parent who sees hard work rewarded where others see only the Trophy That Got Away helps her child define satisfaction a whole lot more broadly, until every all-out effort, no matter what the outcome, is cause for celebration.

Both my parents did a super job on that score. Since I set my own goals unrealistically high, I lost a lot early on. Competitor that I am, blowing a race was catastrophic. I'd be in a real funk afterward, completely absorbed in the task of beating myself up over my failure. At the really difficult age of fourteen, if someone tried to say something nice, I'd blast them for lying. If I announced, "That was the worst race I ever swam," and somebody dared agree with me, I'd burst into tears. At times, no one in my family, not even my mother, could possibly say or do something to save me from beating myself up for not reaching a goal.

But that didn't stop them from trying.

We always went out for pizza with my team after a meet, no matter how badly the meet went, no matter how badly I swam. My family never said, after a particularly jarring defeat, "Well, let's forget about the pizza party, Summer's in no mood for it."

They never said, "Let's just leave her alone for a while till she snaps out of it." They never said, "Summer, cut it out, you're ruining everybody's good time." They didn't try and *say* anything: My dad would put his arm around me and start goofing around, we'd eat pizza with the rest of the team, and inevitably my mood lifted. The whole idea was to remind me that failing to win at a meet wasn't a judgment on my total worth as a human being. So I didn't win! I gave it my best, everyone had enjoyed watching me, now it was over, and there would be a next time when my best might be, in fact, *the* best. Win or lose, we were going to celebrate my trying hard. My attitude became "so I didn't win, pass me the pepperoni."

Don't get me wrong: Winning was definitely motivating, definitely a huge boost to my personal satisfaction quotient. I loved to win, and the more I won, the more motivated I became to put in the work. Rewards, trophies, media coverage, public recognition—you better believe I fed off them. At the age of twelve, I was competing in Junior Nationals; it was in Grand Forks that I had my big breakthrough, winning two individual events and helping my club win the meet. It was a remarkable win in many ways, unique, even, because there were only six of us from CCA—not enough to swim a relay. Since the easiest way to rack up points was to win a relay, this should have been quite a handicap. Yet we still won more points than any other team, so we had our picture taken, all of us wearing these T-shirts my mom had made up that said, "No Relays Required," and we made it into *Swimming World* magazine—a first for me. That was quite a rush, but not nearly as surprising as driving back to The Ambassador and seeing, on a restaurant on the main street, a marquis that said "Congratulations, Summer!" All of Grand Forks, it seemed, had seen me swim, and they bothered to let me know it. It wasn't my first taste of public recognition, but it was the most inspiring.

MY SWIMMING CAREER took off like a rocket with a really long fuse: for years, the spark that was lit when I was four burned along pretty steadily, until suddenly, when I was fifteen, I shot skyward—I darn near made the 1988 Olympic team, a failure that put me on the road to Olympic success. The more athletes I talk to, the more typical this trajectory—the long, slow burn leading up to an explosive takeoff—starts to look. Dan Jansen, Dot Richardson, and Bonnie Blair were all early starters who nonetheless didn't get serious about their sport until they'd put in years trying everything else. Matt Biondi, who everybody assumes was born with gills, actually dreamed of being a basketball star first. He played all different sports as a kid; he joined the Boy Scouts, sang in the choir, took piano and guitar and drum lessons, and of course, swam and played water polo. But for ten years, he took basketball more seriously than swimming, even though he'd won trophies and set records in the pool. Finally, at the age of fifteen, he dropped out of basketball to concentrate on water sports—a move so surprising to his family that his dad asked him if something had happened between him and his basketball coach. Matt had two reasons. He'd begun to appreciate being the best, and it was clear that honor was within his grasp if he stayed in the pool. That's what he told his father. The other reason, which he didn't share with his father: "The other kids made fun of me on the basketball court, because I was skinny and small." The pool was the place where he felt accepted, where he had friends.

Justin Huish, the champion archer, was another one whose rocket didn't take off until he'd explored every sport but archery. He was into baseball, football, tennis, track, basketball, and BMX biking. He wasn't serious about any of them. "I had fun more than I wanted to excel," he notes. As for archery, he'd occasionally join his dad on weekend shoots with a cheap wooden bow he'd been given. Mostly, he helped his parents run their archery store, which they opened when he was fourteen. When a coach his mom had hired to give lessons to local kids on Thursdays asked Justin to come out and give tournament archery a try, Justin refused. "I hated to lose," says Justin. "I didn't want to go out and get stomped on."

Finally, the Thursday-afternoon coach got him to pick up a bow. Justin got pointers on his technique for six weeks before deciding he'd enter the Pumpkin Shoot, a local junior tournament. He won the Pumpkin Shoot. "That's how archery took off for me," says Justin. "It was gratifying from the very beginning."

Of course, as he quickly discovered, it could also be incredibly frustrating: when he entered the next month's tournament, the Turkey Shoot, he couldn't even hit the target. Yet that December—two months after picking up the sport—he shot only ten points off from perfect, earning himself an Olympian patch for his shirt.

"Suddenly, I was so engrossed!" he says. "One day I wasn't into it, the next day I was. Once I got involved, I didn't do anything else."

There's something about that age—fourteen, fifteen—where natural athletes come into their own, *provided* they're allowed to, which I'll explain in a minute. Look at Bonnie Blair: she skates to be with her family, skates competitively for fun, has no experience skating against a clock, and when she's fifteen, decides she'll give clock racing a try right in the middle of the Nationals. "I remember getting out there on the ice and thinking, *What am I doing?*" says Bonnie. "I was all by myself. I kept thinking, *Will I forget to switch lanes on the backstretch?* I had so many things on my mind, not the least of which was knowing that if I came in under forty-seven seconds in the five-hundred, that would give me the qualifying time to go to the [Olympic] trials.

"So the gun goes off, I remember to switch lanes, and at the end of the straightaway, I saw the clock hit forty-two seconds," she continues. "I put my head down, I skated as hard as I could, and I crossed the finish line at forty-six point seven seconds.

"I made a qualifying time my first time out!" Bonnie marvels. "That was the start of it all."

All these athletes, as I see it, took off so spectacularly because no one tried to shorten the fuse, or hurry it along, or set a match to it when it looked like it was all but dead. No parent ever intervened to say, "It's time you got serious about . . ." No parent panicked at what must have looked like a lack of motivation, a lack of direction or focus. No parent tried waving any carrots or big sticks. None of this "If I buy you a bike, will you go to practice?" stuff, or "You'll never get to the Nationals if you don't do double workouts."

For those of us who got an early start—me, Dan, Bonnie, Matt—having our parents gradually recede from the action is what allowed us to feel ownership of our dreams. We grew into the realization that whatever it was we wanted, it was entirely up to us to go after it. By being given ownership of the dream, we were given total responsibility.

A lot of parents are reluctant to give that responsibility—especially in adolescence. It's almost like they say to themselves, "Okay, this experimenting with all different sports and activities has gone on long enough; it's time we get our kid on track, because he's running out of time to be a serious contender." Somehow they lose all faith in their kid's ability to find himself. Or they're too impatient for the discovery process. And that's a shame, because by stepping in to speed things up, they send a no-confidence vote, loud and clear. A child who's entering adolescence, a fourteen- or fifteen-year-old, wants parents to show their support by removing themselves from the discovery process. When you're that age you're desperate to find out who you are by finding out what you can do, and if your parents stay mixed up in it, then there's no knowing where they end and you begin.

Staying out of it may look like disinterest, but in effect, parents who retreat way to the sidelines at this point are saying, in effect, "You can do it. We can see that you have all it takes to get yourself to your goals." That vote of full faith and confidence has the power to motivate a teenager like nothing else.

Look at my friend Karch. Until Karch was fifteen, he and his dad played together as a team (there are only two players on a side in beach volleyball). His dad would set him up, says Karch, and then he'd put it away.

Set. Spike. Score.

I like this image of how a parent should be involved. Karch

and his dad had a bond. They were a team. His dad was the background guy, the enabler; Karch was the rising star, the kid who won the point. When Karch was fifteen, another player—Double A–rated—invited him to play as his teammate in an Open Tournament—something Karch and his dad had never attempted to enter, even though nothing stopped them. Karch's dad said, "I think you should play. You're too good for me. I'd be holding you back if we stayed together."

That was a turning point in every way for Karch, a coming-of-age. He and his new partner finished ninth out of sixty-four teams—a tremendous accomplishment for a player of any age, even the professionals.

"I remember playing the top-seeded guys—and they struggled against us!" he says. "My dad was really proud. He watched every game. We both heard all the buzz—how this local Santa Barbara kid was beating a bunch of grown men. He was seeing me play on a level he'd never seen before, and he was really enjoying having played a part in it."

Fifteen seems to be the coming-of-age year for a surprising number of my athlete friends, as it was for me. That was the year we started to come into our own. We got serious enough about our sport to no longer need quite the level of security blanket our parents' presence had provided. For my friends who were latecomers to their sport, fifteen was not only the age they assumed responsibility for their athletic future, but also the point in their adolescence when they moved from child to adult.

Justin Huish, who also, at fifteen, literally left home to fly around the country and compete in archery tournaments, never doubted his parents' confidence in him, even though it was at arm's length from the start. "They couldn't afford to go with me, but they backed me one hundred percent," he says. "If I needed money, they'd help me out. They never said, 'Are you practicing?' If I said, 'I don't want to shoot,' they'd have said okay. I maintained a regular life; I went off and played my guitar, went snowboarding. They just let me do my thing.

"Not that they didn't put in their advice," he adds. "If I had wanted to fly helicopters, my mom would have let me, even though she thought I was going to die. I remember her saying, 'If you die, I'm going to come up to heaven and kill you again!' "

Norm Bellingham, the world-class kayaker, was drawn to the river at the age of twelve; while his passion was developing, at ages thirteen and fourteen, his parents were in the process of divorcing. By the time their divorce was final, when he was fifteen, he was "fanatical." He'd be out there at dawn, he'd be out there in lieu of P.E. during school, he'd be back at lunch, and in the evening, and instead of doing his schoolwork, he'd be filling in his training log. His parents, both graduates of the University of Chicago, both academics, couldn't understand it. They were a little concerned. They asked him, "Why are you so intense? What is it?" Was this some sort of rebellion? But to their credit, says Norm, they listened to his explanation, and while they didn't get it, they didn't get in the way of it. "They let me find my own way," says Norm. "I was allowed to follow my dreams. They supported me adequately along the way; when I was younger they'd given me the tools, and the mind-set, to pursue excellence, and even when I pushed college out another five years, and seemed to have no hope of financial reward, they supported me. That kind of arm's-length support was critical for my personality type. I'd say to parents, let your kids find their own dream. Don't force your own onto them."

Being allowed to pursue a dream, being allowed to take your own future into your hands, even as an adolescent—the payoff can be huge, and I don't mean just in terms of the sport or activity. I was fanatical about swimming, and that fanaticism took me all the way to the Olympic medal platform, but that energy and motivation and commitment spilled over into my schoolwork, my friendships, and my family. I never failed to do my homework, not because I needed or wanted to be number one, but because I wanted to get into a decent college to be on an excellent swim team with a terrific coach. That, and too many Bs or Cs felt like failure to me. But if it weren't for athletics, I wouldn't have been that insistent on academic excellence.

The fact that I swam and valued my grade performance meant, in turn, I had to make use of every spare minute during the schoolday, because I knew when practice was over I'd be too dead tired to do anything but eat and get to bed. So directly after math period, I'd get out the books and start in on my homework. That solved other difficulties; for one, I couldn't afford to hang out with the kids who were always sneaking off to smoke pot in the bathroom. I'd act as if I couldn't join them because I was already on the verge of real trouble, and cutting class would only make it worse. I was a bit of a mystery because I had this other life no one really understood who wasn't swimming, and I counted on that mystery to help me avoid any number of uncomfortable situations. Kids knew I swam and accepted that it "limited" what I could and could not do outside of practice. That made it easier for me to stay out of stuff I didn't really want to get mixed up in.

Having this thing of value, this life I didn't want to wreck, made it easy to keep the right set of priorities. I never worried about my appearance; I never dieted, I never obsessed about what I ate or what I weighed, I never fussed over makeup or fashion, because these were all nonissues in my world. I can remember going to one junior prom and having twenty minutes to get ready, having just come home from an all-day swim meet. As I tell audiences of high-school girls now, there's more to life than stressing about what shade of pink your nail polish is.

Finally, being a motivated swimmer meant I hung around with other motivated kids, kids who were too high on life to be looking for any other kind of high. My junior and senior years on Friday or Saturday nights, a bunch of us played War Crew, a game we made up. About fifteen guys would meet at Bill Tanner's house, and fifteen girls at Gyenie Gamble's house, whose property backed up to Bill's. The idea was to sneak up through the bushes and pounce on each other (we were all camouflaged in dark clothing and face paint). The first rule was ABSO-LUTELY NO EGGS—so of course, one night the boys showed up with about a hundred eggs. We girls retaliated by going out in pairs, one of us armed with molasses, the other with flour. Somehow, though, the guys always succeeded in turning our own ammo back on us. Some of us were kidnapped in cars, others got thrown in the pond. It was wild. But our parents were not only around, they were involved; Gyenie's dad was the one who blew a whistle and announced, "WAR ON!"

Okay—so maybe we were a *little* unusual.

*   *   *

THE POINT IS, where others would say my motivation paid off in Olympic gold and glory, I felt its payoff all along the way, in innumerable smaller moments shared with my teammates, my friends, my family, the townspeople of Grand Forks, the people I met all over the world. Each little payoff—each breakfast with my dad, each predawn swim with my mom, each prank my brother played, each camper chat with my friends—in turn motivated and inspired me to keep going to practice. Each competition and its adventures added up to keep me pushing, to keep me giving my personal best. The harder I worked, the greater my success, and the more adventures I was invited to be part of, the more memories I forged with friends and family.

That's what I tell the kids I talk to in school auditoriums and malls and stores and swim meets and camps across the country: If I were to hold up one of my medals, what they'd see was the justification for all my 5:15 A.M. practices. But that's backward. What the medal reflects back to me are the countless moments of pure joy along the way. Ultimately, the medals are really just metal.

3

What It Means to Be Supportive

To this day, my mom is afraid people think she was one of those pushy parents I described earlier. After all, she was there on the pool deck, helping out the coach or being a timer. She caught a lot of practices, and she almost never missed a meet. She was even in the pool, swimming competitively.

And when I was little, I used to make her stand at the end of my lane. Not to coach me, not to yell at me. I just wanted the reassurance of her presence.

"Mom," I'd plead, "please, just go stand down there so I can see you."

She'd look around to see if anybody was watching her—like she was about to be caught shoplifting or something—then wander down and take her position. She'd stand there self-consciously, cheering in this little voice, "Go, Summer!"

In the water, I couldn't hear her. I wouldn't necessarily finish the race at her feet, either. But it didn't matter. I knew she was there, and that's all I wanted, all I needed. She was always there for me, even when she was miles away. She knew just how to walk the line between being *reassuring* and being *too involved.*

Parents I talk to want to walk that same line, but aren't sure how. *Should I show up for every practice?* they wonder. *Should I make a big deal out of every win, or play down the victories? Is there such a thing as constructive criticism? And what about quitting? Should I let my child quit if she wants to?*

There's not one right answer, not a simple yes or no to these questions.

Support comes in a variety of sizes and styles. Whereas a four-year-old will need Dad or Mom to be right there, within easy reach of a hug, a teenager might seek out water sports in an effort to claim for herself a world separate from her parents'. Just as in my own experience I needed different things from each parent. I needed my mother to be involved for the very simple reason that I couldn't have kept up with my team's practice schedule without her driving me to and from our pool. And that was enough. I needed my dad to stay out of my swimming life, to give me a life outside of my sport, which he did quite naturally. After talking to my Olympic buddies, I've come to see that we all wanted and needed different kinds of support from our parents, depending on our age, our personality, our parents' inclinations, the nature of our sport, and the absence or presence of other role models or mentors.

And yet, while the support our parents gave looks different in each case, it all comes down to this: They believed in us. They believed we could achieve anything we set our hearts on. They encouraged us to dream big, shoot high, and not be afraid. They put us in the driver's seat, but sat in the back in case we had questions or needed them as a sounding board. Quite simply, they loved us—not for the star athletes we might become, but for the individuals we already were.

Our parents also had similar expectations: They expected us to be nothing less than the best we could be, whatever we determined that was. And we knew that because that was the standard they held themselves to. We could see it, in everything they did, big and small. Not that they were outstanding athletes, or outstanding artists, or outstanding intellectuals themselves, necessarily—it wasn't what they accomplished in their own lives that impressed us, so much as the attitude they brought to whatever they attempted. *Do your best. Pull out all the stops. There's never an excuse for giving anything less.*

Dot Richardson's dad was a retired Air Force senior master sergeant and mechanic. Her mom was a homemaker. While these may seem humble enough occupations, they did everything in their power to do it right.

"My dad took such pride in his job," Dot recalls, "he'd have fixed [cars] for nothing. He never gave up. If he had to get a light out there in the garage and stay up all night, he would. As long as it took to make that engine turn over, he'd give it that effort.

"My mom had the same sense of pride," Dot continues. "Everything she did was neat. You could see it in the way the dishes were dried, or the laundry folded, or the way her bed was made. You could see it in the way she did a church project, or the way she took care of my grandmother up until the very end. Her only frustration was in not having time to do something to her satisfaction."

In that environment, Dot and her brothers and sisters grew

up knowing that whatever they did with their lives, it was going to be a contribution. They were expected to make the world a better place. "That was how my mother approached everything she did," she says. "She gave her best because she felt strongly that it was her duty to leave a place better than she found it."

Karch Kiraly couldn't help but be conscious of his dad's work ethic, even as a little kid. Lying in bed at night, he could hear his father translating tapes from Russian to English for publication in scientific journals—and this was after a long day of medical school—to help support his family. The guy never had a spare moment, according to Karch. He'd worked relentlessly since his own childhood, first to escape Hungary, at the age of twenty-one, then to earn a scholarship to college, then to earn an engineering degree, then to go through medical school. Weekends, when he played volleyball, he brought the same drive, the same doggedness to his game.

"Ultraorganized, focused, dedicated, relentless—that was my dad," says Karch. "He taught me by example."

Norm Bellingham was exposed to excellence early, growing up the middle son in a highly educated household that lived all over the world. His dad's career in the foreign services kept the family in India and Nepal for much of Norm's childhood. Norm met a lot of people "who'd done exciting, wonderful things with their lives"—particularly mountain climbers. Sir Edmund Hillary was an early inspiration. "I wanted to establish myself in a way that was both positive and recognized," Norm says. "I wanted to be seen in the context of doing something unique." That early exposure to achievement, says Norm, gave him the mind-set that would allow him to approach the world "as my own person" later. While his older brother went on to win a Westinghouse Scholarship to MIT, Norm felt he had the tools to pursue excellence on his own terms—in sports, that is, rather than in academics.

My own parents, in terms of their appetite for excellence, were a study in contrasts. Even though my dad was a very successful dentist, it was my mom who really had the drive, who wouldn't allow anything we did to be half-assed, whether it was turning out socks for the laundry or doing our homework. The sad part is, she'd never found, growing up, enough of an outlet for that work ethic. She'd had polio at the age of four, and then encephalitis; her parents thought she was going to die. Then, when she didn't, they were so overjoyed and relieved, didn't push her. She told me she used to go over to her girlfriend's, on Saturdays, to help her do chores, like clean the bathroom and do dishes, just to give herself the structure that no one at home imposed on her. She took ballet after her recovery from polio, both to strengthen her muscles and because she enjoyed the sheer discipline of it. She loved working hard; she was always willing to put in whatever time or effort was necessary to achieve results. She'd work with a show horse on their moves for hours, until she had perfected their performance. But her family didn't understand. They couldn't see why she wanted to push herself, why she wanted to put her body through all that. "My parents babied me," my mother once explained to me. "They didn't realize I *wanted* things to be expected of me."

It was her divorce from my dad that probably finally gave her the opportunity to put all that discipline, hard work, and dedication to work. She had to support us in order to retain custody, and yet she had no job skills, almost no work experience, no college degree, and no network of relatives to pitch in and help her. I can still remember those first months after the divorce was finalized—the three of us living in this run-down house a couple miles from the house my parents had built together. She pounded the pavement looking for a job for six months, taking rejection after rejection, because the stakes were way too high for her to throw up her hands in defeat. She didn't want to lose us. She was prepared to clean houses, if that was the only work she could find. Failure was not an option.

My mom had true grit, raising us with little to no safety net. It left an indelible impression on both Trevor and me. Skills or talent, she showed us during that period, were secondary to having the drive and the determination to make it. She also impressed upon me that whatever my goals, I didn't need to lean on anyone to attain them. "You don't need a man, you don't need money, you don't need anyone else to 'be' somebody," she'd tell me. "You've got everything you need to make your own dreams come true."

Debi Thomas tells almost the exact same story about her mom, who was her only parent growing up. Not enough had been expected of her mother growing up, either, says Debi. She was a brilliant pianist, but wasn't strongly encouraged to take her talent to a competitive level. When she applied to Cornell's electrical engineering program, school advisers advised against it. That's why, Debi believes, her mother always stressed that her own daughter be very goal-oriented. "You may not attain everything," says Debi, "but if you set your expectations high, you're more likely to accomplish something worthwhile."

When Debi was five, she told her baby-sitter she wanted to

become a doctor. "Honey, you can't be a *doctor*," the sitter told her. "You have to be a nurse." Debi shot back, "My mommy said I can be whatever I want to be!"

That was the end of that sitter.

"No way was my mom going to let happen to me what happened to her," says Debi now. "No way would she let me not believe I could do anything."

That is exactly what my mom used to tell me whenever I turned to her for that mental boost that could make all the difference. I never wanted her to do the hard work for me; I wanted her to make me believe I had it in me to take on the challenge myself. So right before a race I'd go up to her and say, "Psych me up, Mom. Tell me something good about myself."

And she'd tell me exactly what I wanted and needed to hear—always some variation on "You're the best! You're the fastest! You can beat that girl, Summer! *You can do whatever you put your mind to!*"

It's a mom thing, I guess. Only a mother can love you so unconditionally that she's blind to all possibility of failure and deaf to any voice of doubt. But as soon as she'd say it, I'd believe it. I'd be psyched. I'd know in the very recesses of my soul that I had the right stuff, that I could overcome whatever odds I was facing.

She didn't *give* me the power; she just reminded me, reassured me, that I already had it, that I could win. Then I *would* win. She confirmed what I already thought: My potential was *infinite*. It was all a matter of tapping into it.

Or rather, it was all a matter of putting my fears aside so they didn't get in the way. It was my mom who'd look at me like she saw my deepest, most hidden worries and then wave them away with a few encouraging words. It wouldn't really matter what words she used; what I came away with was her conviction, which then became my own, because my mom knew me best, and if she thought I had nothing to fear, then it must be true. She would never lie to me. When she said, "You're the best," it wasn't because I'd just won a race, or because I had shelves of trophies, or because I'd broken a record. It was a blanket statement about me, regardless of what I did or accomplished. And when she said, *"You can do whatever you put your mind to,"* that wasn't wishful thinking, but a fact she had proven to herself and demonstrated to me and Trevor every day that we lived with her.

During those six months we lived under her roof, my mom had no life outside of keeping ours together. Trevor and I were latchkey kids, but it never felt that way to us. We'd come home to a house peppered with little notes that said stuff like "Don't forget to lock the door!" or "Hope you had a wonderful day!" Sometimes we'd go home with a friend or my dad would pick me up until it was time for swim practice. I had practice every afternoon at five. My mom would drive across town like a maniac to gather me up and race to whatever part of town my club had rented that season—it changed a lot, our pool locale, until I was fourteen. Either Trevor came with us, or he'd go to soccer practice and then home with a friend. Usually my mom would hang out and watch me practice. Or she'd use the time to get groceries. Occasionally she went back to her office, or did paperwork in her car. As soon as practice was over, we'd pick up Trevor and race home so she could get dinner going. After dinner, for us, it was homework before bed; for my mom, it was dishes, laundry, bills to pay, garbage to take out.

In high school, when swim practice became part of my morning routine, my mom got up with me at 4:14 A.M., drove me to Sacramento for 5:15 A.M. practice, hung out with me there, and then dropped me off at school before showing up at her office, which by then was in real estate. Afternoons, I carpooled. Trevor had soccer, or swim practice, or a part-time job after school. Our days with my mom were regimented, partly because her six-month custody happened to span the school year, partly because my sport was so time-intensive, and partly because, of course, my mom was a single working mother. She simply didn't have the time or money to be care-free, not the way my dad was. She used to joke that if someone failed to unload the dishwasher, her whole day would fall apart.

But we didn't mind the routine, the regimentation. We had chores, but looking back on them, they didn't seem like much. We had to clean the bathrooms, Trevor and I. We did our laundry so we'd have clean clothes, and we packed our lunches so we'd have something to eat at lunchtime. We didn't feel oppressed. My mom was doing all she could.

Cutting out my swimming would have definitely lightened her load, in terms of both time and money. Yet she felt strongly, always, that the least she could do as our mom was honor our commitments. I was dedicated to swimming, she could see that: I hated to miss practice, or be late for it. If I was going to be committed enough to get up and get into the car by 4:25 A.M., then she felt the least she could do was get up with me and drive me over there.

"I never resented the sacrifices," she insists. "You were my priority. I *did* resent feeling guilty about constantly having to choose, choose between you and something else—going to work, going grocery shopping, going to one child's meet, not being able to be in two places at once.

"I never thought the whole push was for nothing," she explains. "But it was never about those medals on the wall. What was important was what kind of adults you were going to grow up to be."

EVEN WHEN SHE couldn't be literally there, my mom would be a presence. Those notes Trevor and I came home to in grade school, for instance—she was always writing us little pep talks. I'd open my lunch at school and there'd be her handwriting on a scrap of paper. "Hope you're having a good day!" it'd say, or "Study hard!" The message between the lines was always, *You're in my thoughts, because I love you so much.* She never stopped writing them.

Later, when I was away from home, I'd pick up the phone to get that precious reassurance. It wasn't so much that I needed psyching up; I just needed to feel like I had nothing to fear, and only my mom could make me feel that way. I can remember calling home after my first week at Stanford, when I'd just discovered how really brilliant everybody was. I was scared to death. "Oh my God, Mom," I bawled, "I can't do this! They're so smart and I'm so dumb—how am I going to do this? They were all valedictorians! I can't compete with these people! I'M NEVER GOING TO MAKE IT!"

"Now, Summer," she had said, all calm, "you were an honors math student and you got good grades and that was all while you were swimming mornings, afternoons, and Saturdays! Did any of those girls do that? Were they on the student council, too? Are they as nice as you are?"

She could have just dismissed my feelings as hysteria ("Oh, you'll be just fine—give it a week or two!"). Or she could have decided the problem was so big she had to offer solutions or step in and handle it herself ("We'll get you a tutor!"). But she didn't; she listened. She took me seriously; she helped me break down the wall I was facing into manageable little hurdles; and she offered, as always, her most sincere reassurance I had everything I needed to get on top of this problem.

"I felt so awful for you," she's shared with me since, "that I could hardly bear it, just listening. I wanted to step in, I wanted to fix this for you. But that wouldn't have helped you. I'd have been getting in the way of any emotional or mental or physical growth you were going through.

"My job," my mom told me, "was simply to *be there for you* in your journey, Summer. Whatever that was."

And she managed to, even when I couldn't call her, even when she couldn't be there with me. She'd find a way to shuttle me messages, usually through a chain of other swimmers and coaches, sometimes by mail, once, even, via a stewardess on a United Airlines flight. They were usually these jokey little poems she'd written about swimming. Here's one I still have:

Ode to Summer's 400 IM
by Momma

One little poem to help you get thru the day
About being your best in every way

You're a sweetheart & polite and gentle and kind
But get you on the blocks and there's only racing on your mind.

When the horn sounds you get a great start
Your butterfly leg puts you on top of the chart.
During the backstroke, Kristina will be there,
But you don't slow down, you don't even care.

Breaststroke is yours from beginning to end
You're so powerful and you move like the wind.
Only 2 more laps are left till you're through,
And with all your hard work, I know you can do!!

If you're happy with your time and happy with your race,
Then it really doesn't matter what was your place.

I know you want to win, because I would too.
But the most important thing you see,
Is to be the very *best you can be.*

And with that in mind, everyone else is in trouble,
Because here comes Summer on the double.
She's strong, mean, *and has fire in her eyes*
And she's so tall, she can touch the skies!

She has places to go and things to do,
And she doesn't quit until she's through.

This is kind of long, and it took lots of time,
So I better stop now, before I run out of rhymes.

But one last thing before this stops,
In my book, I KNOW you are tops!!!

20 July 1992

Her poetry wouldn't win any prizes. But the thought behind it had a lot to do with my prizes.

Family Support

My mom was the most involved in my swimming. She knew all my times; she knew my coaches; she knew Who Was Who among the competition; she knew the sport inside and out. That was her choice. That was her pleasure.

Yet the rest of my family was also there for me, in ways not as obvious, maybe, but certainly as important.

My dad, as I've said, felt it was his mission to provide balance. It's true he didn't like the way my swimming got in the way of his plans for fun, but he came to my meets, and he gave me what my mother could not—a chance to take myself less seriously. A former athlete himself, he knew all about the pressure I felt; it was his responsibility to try and lighten me up before a big race. "Make sure you breathe," he'd say, perfectly straight-faced. "Make sure your suit is on." The closest he could come to being serious, before a race, was to say, "Go, Summer!" in this quick, deep voice. But typically he'd just hug me and try to get my mind off what was ahead. Even when I was competing in the 1992 Olympics, my dad took what little chance we had to communicate to ask me all about the Olympic Village— not one word about my swimming, even though he was proud as hell of my accomplishment.

When I was younger, and the stakes weren't as high, my father didn't come to every meet. Later, he'd come to my meets, but sometimes he'd miss my performance altogether. Not on purpose, not for lack of trying—maybe it was just bad luck. I could usually keep my eye on him during the meet because he wasn't up in the stands with everybody else—he was down in the photographers' pit. Invariably he'd have sweet-talked someone into giving him a press pass, just so he could see me up close. My dad would be standing around with camera guys from NBC and photographers from the *Los Angeles Times,* wearing his official *Sacramento Bee* tag and taking snapshots of me with his Kodak Instamatic. So when he'd take a moment to step outside and get a cup of coffee or light a cigarette, I'd know it. And later, I'd nail him for it.

"How was my race?" I'd say. "Did you see me?"

For half a second he would toy with the idea of pretending he'd seen me, just so as not to hurt my feelings. I'd seen him try that with other people: One time, while we were attending the 1984 Olympics in Los Angeles, he spotted one of the swimming dads he knew, a guy whose son had made the Olympic team, and he yelled out, "Your son did GREAT!"—as if my dad had seen his kid compete. The guy looked at us kind of dumbfounded. "Uh, no Bob," he said. "My son pulled his hamstring." His son was expected to win gold and actually came in sixth.

But my dad could never lie to me. "Aw, Summer!" he'd say, chuckling with frustration—he'd be so pissed. Down there the whole day and he picked that one moment to go to the bathroom and miss me. "I can't believe it!" he'd say. "I'm so sorry. How'd ya do?"

And I always said, "Great, Dad." Because even if he'd seen me, he wouldn't have known bad from good. He didn't know my times, he wouldn't have had the foggiest notion of whom I was up against. Which was fine with me, because at times my mom knew too much. Just by being himself, he provided the kind of support I needed in my sport.

Maybe more important, my dad provided the support I needed *outside* of swimming. He had terrific radar for when Trevor and I were in need of someone to just sit down and listen. Divorce may have given him that radar; it was almost as if he realized he'd blown it once by failing to communicate, and now he wasn't about to let that kind of divide spring up with his kids. I asked him once, "How come Mom was the one who told us you were getting a divorce?"

"I don't remember, really," he said slowly, "but I do remember she was really emotional, and I was out of town, and she took it upon herself . . . well, she acted on a whim. It probably happened like that."

"Or could it be," I persisted, "that you felt like you failed, for being the child of a divorced family yourself?"

"That could be," he said, like he was turning over that possibility for the first time. He admitted to me he did feel like a failure, getting divorced, because his own parents had, and he'd sworn he wouldn't. He's not an introspective guy, my dad, but divorce opened his eyes—and his ears—to a lot.

He'd try and be there for me not just as a father but as a mother, too. I can remember procrastinating on an art assignment until it was the night before it was due and I hadn't even started it. I had to sew a sock that was filled with sand, and put a face on it. I was afraid to go to my dad for help; I thought he'd be mad at me for leaving it until the last minute. And then, of course, I thought there was no way he could help. What did he know about sewing? But I was desperate. I asked him for help, and he got all into it—he went to town on that stupid sock. "Let's put some color on there," he said. "How 'bout blue eyes? Red lips! And how 'bout this gold paper—we could make a crown!"

I still have that ratty sock. He sewed it, and he did a fine job.

Even when I hit puberty, and didn't think I could survive being the only chick in a house of guys, my dad was there for me. He was an expert at coaxing out what I wanted to say, needed to say, but couldn't say, not without help.

"What's the matter?" he'd ask me, seeing me unusually somber.

"Nothing," I'd sulk.

"Aw, come on," he'd insist. "I know there's something wrong." He would continue this way until I finally told him what it was. Sometimes this could go on for quite a while, but he wouldn't let me hold out on him.

When I was a junior in high school, I remember coming home to my dad's from school on the verge of a breakdown because some boy I'd had a crush on had given me the total brush-off. My dad was holding, as he often did, a business meeting at home. We knew to be quiet. But when I went into my room, I found Chip, my black Lab puppy, sitting on the floor with chewed-up bits of my favorite bathing suit around him. It wasn't really Chip's fault; I hadn't spent enough time with him to train him. So I'd put him in my room because he was out of control. And he'd torn my bikini to shreds.

I went ballistic—out of all proportion to the incident. "BAD

DOG!" I shrieked. "I CANNOT *BELIEVE* YOU!" I was bawling. I completely forgot about my dad's meeting.

Next thing I know, my dad's in my doorway. "What is your *problem?*" he asked.

I explained to him about Chip. And then, before I knew it, I blurted out what was really bothering me.

He sat down. He went from being angry to asking me to take my time and tell him all about this guy at school. Because he just listened, and didn't interrupt, he didn't have to pry it out of me. Then, when I'd poured out everything completely, waiting for my dad to say something fatherly, or give me advice, he leaned forward and said, "Well, it's his loss completely. He's gonna come back in a year and say, 'Damn! Why didn't I nab that one when I had the chance!' "

He could always make me smile. It's what he did best.

His usual response—to never take anything too seriously— was also just what I needed. So one day, when I was in sixth grade, over at a friend's house, we got to playing around with her clothes and agreed we needed training bras. Her mom called up my dad, to ask his permission, and he laughed. "May as well get one for me, that's about how much she needs it—what are they training?" But he knew how important it was for me and I came home wearing this thing, size negative A. "Feel my back!" I said to Dad and Trevor. I was so excited. They both started laughing so hard, I wanted to hide. I knew if my mom were there, she would have said something like "Now, don't make fun, Bob, this is an important moment." But she wasn't. And almost immediately, I started thinking, *This* is *pretty stupid.* I never wore that bra again.

Living at my dad's, I had to laugh at myself. I had to see

things from his and Trevor's perspective, or I had to remind myself, *They don't know: they're guys!*

Trevor in particular kept me in line, off the pedestal that my swimming successes might have put me on, by reminding me he had Absolute Power. One time he won an entire box of chewing gum at a dental convention we'd gone to with my father. Would he give me a pack? Would he give me even *one piece?* No way—not until I agreed to give him my favorite teddy bear. My most cherished stuffed animal, for two lousy packs of gum! But I did it, of course. And as soon as I gave him my toy, he threw it under his bed. All along it was about Power, not some stupid stuffed animal he couldn't have cared less about. Another time he got an autograph from Billy Simms, a football player we both admired; he was going to copy it and sell it. I paid him twenty-five cents for a copy and I felt lucky to be let in on this hot property. He had high hopes for selling more but I don't think he sold a single other copy. I was the only sucker. As I got older, and more sensitive about my appearance, he'd exploit that weakness, too. All he'd have to say to me was, "You're wearing *that?*" and I'd rush back to my room to change. Or I'd be getting ready for a prom or some date and he'd say, "Is that a mosquito bite? No . . . it's a *zit!*"

Yet for all that torture, my brother was my closest ally, my best friend, my confidant, and always my biggest fan. I remember when he taught me to play basketball when I was about twelve. He showed me how to dribble, how to do a layup, and I was so bad—I'd dribble the ball off my foot, I'd miss the hoop entirely. But he'd say, "Man, Summer, you could be Cheryl Miller! You have such a talent! You should go out for the team!" And when I was swimming and he wasn't (he had a lot of talent, but he was interested in a lot of other things), he'd come to my meets and do his own psych-me-up routine. Just before I was to get up on the blocks, he'd come up to me, put both hands on my shoulders, and say, in his best Obi-wan Kenobe voice: "May the Force be with you." And just as seriously, I'd respond, "And also with you." Then we'd both crack up. This was our prerace ritual. It meant a tremendous amount to me.

Not that there wasn't plenty of sibling rivalry. One occasion in particular I'll never forget: We were in the car, heading over to my cousins' house. I forget what spurred it, but Trevor was in a terrible mood. My dad really wanted to know what was bugging him. "Anything you want to talk about?" he pressed. "Summer's swimming bothering you?" Trevor kept saying no, until suddenly he choked out, "I'm sometimes jealous. Yeah, I am." My parents told him they understood and that they didn't blame him. Then it was okay. He needed to just say it. Trevor wasn't involved in any one thing the way I was with swimming. My parents leaped on anything he got into—soccer, even swimming—but it wasn't his personality to latch on to one thing and be totally consumed by it. Trevor knew that. So maybe he was jealous, but I don't think resentful. He and I were just different.

In fact, he managed to make me jealous of him. We'd go to swim meets and Trevor made it seem like he had the better time, even though he had no choice but to come. Sometimes he would play golf while I was at a meet. My dad would drop him off at a course or stick around and play with him and Trevor would usually beat him. Or the two of them would hook up with a baseball card convention, or go find an arcade, or take in a movie. Other times Trevor would come to the meet and help the coach with the timing. He could make friends in a millisecond, and no matter where we went, his friends seemed to be there waiting for him.

For years, he had this thriving pin-trading business at meets. I was probably most jealous of that. Trevor may have single-handedly started the whole Club Pin collecting mania. Each swim club had its own pin, and pins got to be really big as collectibles. Once, in Barcelona, I gave a cabdriver one and he waived my fare. Anyway, Trevor'd be out there in the stands with his tackle box, all his pins neatly arranged on little foam inserts, and he'd get so involved in the business he couldn't be dragged away. When I'd look at my own pathetic collection (pinned to a towel), I'd wish I was in the stands instead of in the pool. I hated missing out on anything Trevor was passionate about, and even though I was passionate about swimming, and competing, his passions always felt like something I'd like even better.

He might have been jealous of my success, but he wouldn't let me feel that way. He was proud of me. When he ran for class office his senior year, his posters said, "Vote for Summer's brother!" And he was protective of me; when I got off the bus after winning my first medal, it was Trevor who steered me to safety through a mob of people waiting for me. In college, he lived with me at Stanford for a semester as my agent's intern. He was in it for the business experience, of course, but he did it for me, and at a huge personal cost—he'd broken up with his girlfriend, Jenny, the woman who would eventually become his wife, to go on the road with me. He traveled with me on all my endorsement jobs, keeping me on track, keeping me company, keeping me from messing up. I counted on him for his business sense, for his level head. If I needed to know, "Is this agent a slimeball or what? Is he going to deliver on all these promises?" Trevor knew the answer. Even with my own parents, he'd be the go-between, the one who'd assure them, "Summer knows what she's doing."

We had an understanding, even when we were young. We had a pact to take care of each other. For all the power he had to ditch me or crush my ego on the spot, he never used it when what I most needed was his support. Likewise, I looked out for him. For instance, on the days we moved from one parent's house to the other's, we never had to say much. Just a look, just a wink was enough. We'd climb out of the car together and head inside to unpack and fix up our rooms. I plastered my walls with Michael Jordan posters and magazine pictures. Trevor had baseball and soccer stars on his. We'd come in to each other's room and flop on the bed and offer opinions on how the decor was coming along. At some point, even though we didn't talk about it, we'd go out and call whichever parent we had just left, to check on them. We were always thinking the same thing on those occasions: *How's Dad (or Mom) doing, all alone?*

Once, when we were about twelve and fourteen and living with my mom, we all went over to my dad's house because my mom had to talk to him about money. Trevor and I were told to stay outside. We found a tennis ball and threw it up on the roof, over and over, trying to outguess each other about where it would roll off. We were standing out front, waiting for the ball to appear, when we heard this bloodcurdling scream. The front door burst open and out rushed Mom, screaming her head off like we had never heard her.

I was so scared, I didn't know what to think. I looked at Trevor, and he looked at me, and even though I knew he was as worried as I was, he didn't freak. "They're arguing, that's all," he said with this incredible, reassuring calm. "Don't worry— Mom is not going to take us from Dad." When there was no one else to turn to, he was like a parent to me. When I didn't know what to do, when I didn't know how to act or react, I'd turn to Trevor.

In 1998 one time I shared a car ride with a producer. It was a long trip, so he started telling me about his own kids, a son and daughter. He'd recently gotten divorced. The son lived with him, the daughter with her mother maybe three hours away. While he was talking, I started thinking about how difficult it must be for that brother and sister.

"I think that you should know how important a sibling is— especially in this situation," I said. "Maybe it's you and your ex-wife, but they should really have each other. You should be making that sacrifice—they shouldn't have to."

"Gee," he said. He was genuinely shocked. "I never looked at it that way."

I couldn't believe I'd blurted that. But I couldn't *not* speak up. I couldn't let him think it was okay, this arrangement he had. I couldn't have survived without Trevor. Things would have been very different.

Hands-off Parenting

Trevor and I were given a lot of rein growing up. Our parents let us learn on our own, even if that meant we learned the hard way. Our parents let us make our own decisions, even if we screwed up. Were we ready for all that responsibility? No. But that was the point. We'd never be ready if we weren't allowed to practice. By letting us screw up in little ways early on, our parents spared us from screwing up in big ways later on, when the cost would have been a lot higher.

Twice, for instance, I decided to quit swimming. Not for any good reason, really—but that's what I figured out for myself. When I was about ten, I stopped going to practice because I thought I might be missing out on stuff that was more fun. I told my parents I wanted to come home after school like everybody else did, watch a little TV and just hang out. I thought a whole world of opportunity would open up if I didn't have to rush out of school to swim two hours, eat dinner, do my homework, organize my stuff for the following day, and get to bed by nine.

I learned pretty quickly that TV was boring. The two hours I thought represented a huge chunk of time to do other things turned out to fly by with nothing to show for it, day after day. I missed my swimming friends. I missed my coach. I missed all the nervous excitement I felt before a race. I missed the good feeling that came from doing something I did extremely well.

What's funny is that my dad—the one who was probably thrilled I wasn't going to swim practice anymore—was the one who got me swimming again, by taking me and Trevor to the 1984 Olympics. He wanted us to feel what it was all about. He took us to Los Angeles that summer, and Trevor and I had the vacation of our lives. We didn't care what we held tickets for, we didn't care whose autograph we got, as long as I got my American flag signed. That's when I announced, "I'm so PSYCHED! I want to go back to swimming!"

When I was twelve, I tried out for junior high cheerleading and I made the squad. That meant I had to show up at the football games, which took place during swim practice. I quit swimming.

My mother said fine and allowed me to find out for myself that cheerleading was definitely not worth giving up swimming.

I was the *worst* cheerleader. First of all, I looked anything but cute: I'd ordered a child's size 12 uniform because I was such a matchstick, and they sent me a *woman's* size 12. My grandmother put elastic in the waist—as if that would help. Secondly, although I knew football, somehow there were too many distractions. And from our repertoire of ten cheers, we always picked the wrong one. And finally, I couldn't remember the chants. During one pep rally, we seventh-graders were trying to out-yell the eighth-graders, who had just finished doing their version of the spirit chant. We had our own version, which my fellow cheerleaders were shouting in unison. But not me. I belted out the eighth-graders' chant, so loud I didn't even realize my mistake until everybody else died down and I was out there shouting this thing in front of the entire school all by myself.

It was beyond embarrassing. Cheerleading was clearly not where God had intended me to use my gifts.

But the real reason I kept coming back to swimming was that everything I loved revolved around it. I loved to swim fast, I loved to compete, I loved winning huge trophies, I loved the friends the sport gave me, I loved to travel, I loved the times it gave me with my mom, my dad, and my brother, and after that trip to see the '84 Games, I loved fantasizing about going all the way. All the way to the Olympics.

Handling me in one of my quitting phases, my mother says, was a lot like handling a runaway horse. If either she or my dad were to pull hard on the reins—as in, "You better be focusing on the Olympics!"—I wouldn't have stopped running away, I just would have become more frantic about escaping. But when my parents let go of the reins entirely, I decided on my own to stick to the trail. It was the ultimate confirmation of what they were always telling me: I had all that I needed to reach any goal I had in mind; it was all up to me what I made of myself.

But in return for all this free rein, my parents—my mother, I should say—absolutely insisted that if I was going to make the decisions, I had to be held accountable for their outcome. That was the price of independence. She wasn't going to step in and spare me any more than she was going to step in and make a decision for me.

Matt Biondi notes that his parents did the same thing with him and his brother and sister. "They supported our initiatives, our decisions—within guidelines," he says. "If I wanted to play the guitar, for example, they'd say, okay, we'll rent a guitar. But if suddenly I wanted to quit, my mom would say, 'Now, wait a minute, you really wanted to do this, we've paid for it, you're going to give it a fair try.' They always held me accountable for my decisions. As long as they could see I was making an honest effort, living up to my word, fulfilling obligations, they'd let me do whatever it was I wanted to do. They never really stepped in. They never really had to: we were good kids, I think because they trusted and expected us to be."

When I was thirteen, I tested my freedom at a party at my dad's house. He was always one to host these swim-team bashes where all the parents had ungodly amounts of wine and beer. On this one occasion, I don't know what came over me, but I saw a bottle of wine on the table and grabbed it. Another kid and I then went back to my room and downed the entire thing as fast as we could. We were so proud of ourselves, we couldn't wait to see what some of the older crowd would say, so we shared our secret with a select few . . . and then went into the pantry and got another bottle.

I was already absolutely trashed. A lot of the older kids, feeling protective, came in and tried to take care of me, but I was vomiting, and it was very obvious something was going on. My dad came in, grabbed me, sat me down on the toilet, and said, tapping out each syllable on my sternum, "Are—you—DRUNK?!"

I couldn't even hold my head up. Everything was floating from side to side.

For days I was punished, but not by my parents. The next day, Dad made me go on all his errands in the car, exaggerating the swerving and the stopping and asking me, in a really loud voice, "SO! HOWYA FEELIN' TODAY!"

"I don't know what you're talking about," I'd say. "I feel absolutely fine."

But he wasn't buying it. "THINK YOU'RE EVER GOING TO DRINK AGAIN?" he'd shout, and slap me on the back.

Then I had to face everybody who'd been at the party, including my coach and all the older kids I had wanted to impress. I thought Mike, my coach, would be really mad at me, but when I walked into practice he started snickering—and that was worse. All the other kids, too, laughed at me. Whenever I'd see their parents, I'd get bright red with embarrassment, because I knew they were all remembering "the incident."

There was one other learning experience I would never in a million years want to repeat. My mom and I were going on a much-anticipated vacation to Mexico. This was incredibly special because my mom was always financially strapped; it was our dad who took us on vacations. But she had saved up, and we were planning on getting a very-early-morning flight out of San Francisco, which was three hours' drive away. The night before, however, was my best friend Heather's party at her health club, and even though I wasn't much of a partyer, I wanted to go.

I was seventeen. All my mother said was "Be outside at three A.M., because we have to make that flight. I don't want any complications."

There were a lot of boys there doing beer bongs, chugging it through this device that sent the beer to your stomach all at once. I was trying to be cool, so I joined them. Before I knew it, I was in a bathroom stall, throwing up. The whole party shut down early because everybody was too drunk. Heather took me to a friend's house near the club, put me to bed, and set the alarm clock.

The next thing I know, I'm seeing *4:00* A.M. on the clock face.

Sheer panic.

Meanwhile, of course, my mother has roused everybody she could think of from a dead sleep: my brother, my father, my friends' parents. By the time I made it to the health club parking lot, they were all there. "Summer," my mother said, "I'm so mad I can't even talk to you."

We had missed all chance of making the Club Med charter. My mom made a lot of calls and found a flight out of Sacramento that would get us to Phoenix in time to catch up with our plane. We drove in silence to the airport with me a little hungover, to say the least, and my mom so upset I expected her to turn around any minute and cancel the whole trip.

Finally she turned to me. "Summer," she said, "we've both worked too hard for this vacation to have the whole thing ruined now. I'm not going to stay angry. But don't you *ever* do this again."

Dot remembers causing her dad similar pain by being similarly irresponsible. She and her brothers, Kenny and Lonnie, had made themselves javelins out of bamboo sticks and then competed with each other to see who could throw one the farthest. That wasn't so bad. But to make the spears go even farther, they got some of their dad's drill bits—which they knew they weren't supposed to touch—and stuck them in the ends.

"I can remember thinking, as Lonnie threw his spear," Dot told me, " 'Don't hit Dad's new windshield!' Then I threw mine—and it landed dead center in Dad's hundred-dollar windshield."

Dot says Kenny, her older brother, went over to the car, pulled the spear out, took off the drill bit, and stuck the spear right back in the windshield. No sense in making matters worse than they already were.

Dot's punishment was to do the dishes, without her sisters' help, for an entire month. She hated doing them; it had always seemed unfair to her that the girls wound up cleaning up after the meals while the guys watched the football game on TV. But that month, she never grumbled. She would have done them forever, she says, if she thought she could undo the windshield business. It was the guilt she felt for causing her dad this disappointment, which he didn't deserve in the least. He never commented on it, though; he knew he didn't need to.

Although my mom did make me pay for the extra tickets from Sacramento, she kept her word—there was no grudge-bearing, no "I told you so." She knew I'd learned my lesson. She didn't ground me, didn't take back my driving privileges, literally or figuratively. She knew I'd drive more responsibly after that crash. No matter how high the stakes, my parents continued to entrust them to me. They supported my decisions, even when they saw I was pained by them, even when they might not have made the same decisions for me. Their attitude was never "You should have listened to me." Instead, it was "You tell me how I can support you while you handle the consequences of your decision."

Since I had given up my eligibility in 1992, I decided to commentate on the 1993 NCAA championships; I was twenty. Commentating was part of the new career I had chosen in broadcasting—but it was so weird for me to be talking about swimming, fully clothed, while my teammates went at it the way I used to. I'd been Stanford's NCAA champion. I'd come away from them with six individual titles during my freshman and sophomore years.

I called my mom; I begged her to come and be there with me. I was filled with doubt about my decision to leave swimming. "Mom," I remember sobbing, back at the hotel, "did I do the right thing? Did I make the right decision?"

And as always—whether or not she thought my decision was the right one—my mom listened and calmed me with her unquestioning faith. Whatever decision I made, she told me, she'd support it because it was mine to make and she knew I would have given it careful thought and thorough examination.

I was trusted to make what few decisions had to be made, on the premise, I think, that I probably *would* screw up—and learn more from that than anything my parents tried to teach me. "You're in the driver's seat," my mom said repeatedly. She gave me the car, the keys, and her trust full well knowing that I was headed for some fender benders, or perhaps even a crash—but also knowing there was no better way to teach me how to negotiate the trickier turns and dangerous curves down the road.

Critical of My Behavior, Not Me

Good parenting is not just knowing when to keep quiet. It's also knowing when to speak up.

Dot Richardson remembers making an error that cost her teammates a shot at the championship title. The bases were loaded, and Dot, the shortstop, bungled the ball. The girl on third base scored. Dot's team lost.

"On the way home, in the car, I'm bawling my eyes out," says Dot, "and my dad says to me, 'What are you crying for?'

" 'You saw it! I lost the game for us!' I cried. My dad shook his head. 'Listen,' he told me. 'When you're on the field, you do it or you don't. Tonight, you just didn't do it. But you won't let it happen again. You'll practice harder.' "

Dot realized he was right. "I realized at that moment I was going to work harder so it never happened again," she recalls.

Her mother reacted very differently to these outbursts. Dot remembers calling her mom in Orlando from a game she'd just helped her team lose in Arizona—a regional game that would have put them in competition for the Nationals if they'd won. " 'Mom,' I sobbed, 'I made an error, the run counted, we lost—and here I am, UCLA's big recruit! I blew it for us to get to the Nationals!' And she said, 'Dot, I'm sure it wasn't just your fault! I know you tried your best!'

"She'd tell me what I wanted to hear," Dot says. "My dad would tell me the way it *was*."

There's something about the car trip home from a big meet or game that makes for these moments. Dan Jansen recalls driving home with his dad after placing second in his first national championship—an event he had expected to win, at the age of twelve. "I cried all the way home," says Dan. "I kept waiting for my dad to say something; he was the kind of guy who would tell you what you needed to hear without saying a lot. Well, he said nothing the whole ride home. Then he takes me in the house, sits me down—I felt sure I was about to be relieved of my burden—and he says, 'Dan, there's more to life than skating around in a circle.' "

It wasn't what he expected to hear, says Dan. But it was what he needed to be told.

Our parents were consistently *parental;* it was not their job to tell us how to play our game or skate our routine or swim our race. It was not their job to improve us as athletes. It was definitely their job, however, to improve us as human beings. If they stepped out of their passive role in the stands and into our competitive field of play, it was because they took issue with our behavior, not our performance.

Matt Biondi recalls the one time his mother stepped out of the stands and literally stepped onto the court.

"I was playing in a tennis tournament," he recollects. "It was in the middle of the end round, and I was getting beat, so I started slamming my racket on the net and stomping around to show everybody how mad I was at the whole match. Next thing I know, there's my mom, walking up to me at the service line. She doesn't say a thing, she just takes me by the ear—literally, by the ear—and drags me off the court, in front of all those people. She didn't let go all the way to the car. She never said a word all the way home.

"What's always been important to both my parents is how I play the game, not whether or not I win," says Matt. "If my mom doesn't know all that much about swim times or records, it's because she's paying attention to *me,* rather than my performance."

My mother knows all my times, and knows an awful lot about swimming. But I'd have to agree with Matt: it's me she's watching, it's me she's there for, it's me she's concerned about, as her child, as an evolving adult. If I won, but I swam poorly, she'd remind me that I didn't give my best. And if I lost, and took my loss poorly, she wouldn't let me get away with being a poor sport.

One Fourth of July weekend when I was seven years old I swam in a "long-course" meet, meaning every event was at least fifty meters, or one length of an Olympic-size pool. I was feeling really cocky, because I was seeded first in virtually every event— no one came even close to my times. "Lemme see the program," I kept saying to everybody, as though I didn't already know where I stood. Anyway, for the freestyle race, I felt I was in such good shape timewise that I could afford to take it easy, so I did—breathing only on one side—and my mom could see it.

Until the very end, I thought I had the race nailed. But just as I reached for the wall, I saw this girl a couple lanes over touch me out.

God, I was near tears I was so pissed.

"The timers are wrong!" I blurted to my mother. "I was swimming my fastest! There's something wrong with the timers!"

But she turned to me with this little smile on her face and said, "You just didn't see her, did you, Summer?"

And I hadn't. As soon as my mom said that, I couldn't believe I'd come out with that line about the timers.

"You thought you could be lazy and win this event," my mother continued. "I saw you out there. I could tell when you noticed her, I could see your arms go faster."

My mom put her arm around me. "Summer," she said, "you're going to have to earn it every time. It's never in the bag. There's always someone out there ready to beat you, so don't get up on that high horse. You're only going to get knocked down."

THAT'S THE CLOSEST thing to criticism I ever heard from my mom. "Remember," she'd remind me whenever I got a little smug about my performance, "anybody could beat you any day of the week." I can't remember a negative word about me, only the negative reaction to my behavior on those few occasions when I really let my parents down, character-wise.

More often than not, they'd try to *protect* me from criticism: On his first day as our new coach, Mike Hastings bawled me out for being late. My mom immediately stepped in. "If Summer's late for practice, it's because I'm late getting out of work," she told him. "This kid is always ready, and always on time, so if she's late you talk to me about it." Another time, a teacher gave me a detention for chewing gum as I was leaving school. My mom marched into the principal's office and said, "You've got an honors student who wasn't even chewing during school hours. Detention's a waste of her time, and I'm not going to allow her to serve it!"

My parents were eager to support me, defend me, and praise me for anything I took on seriously, which is to say, they always applauded honest effort. And I was usually deserving, because I pushed myself hard. Even if my performance was less than winning, my effort was almost always all out, and that's what they rewarded.

But then there was the year I turned fourteen—the year my parents found it almost impossible to support, defend, or praise me, because I wasn't making much of an effort in anything. I was so emotional, they found it difficult to even *talk* to me. After a race I'd done poorly in I'd stamp my foot and pout. "That was the *worst,* that was *awful,*" I'd say—and if my mom agreed, "You're right, that wasn't one of your best times," I'd turn on her and scream, "Oh, what do you know! You don't know anything! That was only one bad swim!"

My mom didn't know what to do with me that year. She admits to me now, that was the one year she felt she totally floundered as a parent. Yet she took my feelings and concerns seriously. Never once do I remember her cutting me off in the middle of an emotional outpouring by saying, "It's just your hormones speaking," or, "You're getting all bent out of shape over absolutely nothing." My dad, too—he didn't try to wash his hands of me, even though I gave him plenty of reason to want to. He paid for a sports psychologist to come and talk to me. My dad couldn't figure out what my problem was, but he was willing to spend the money on someone else who might, someone who might be there in ways my dad acknowledged he could not.

Both my parents struggled to make their support unconditional. But I sure didn't make it easy. It was almost as if I were testing them, pushing their limits, wanting to behave in some way that would relieve me of responsibility for my decisions.

And what I learned was, their support of *me* was unconditional, but in terms of putting up with *my behavior*—they quickly showed me their limits.

My dad had no trouble speaking his mind. I remember him confronting me at a Los Angeles swim meet. I'd been a complete wiseass—everything he said, I sneered at. Finally, he sat me down. "Look," he said. "I took off work to come down here for four days. I've spent a ton of money on a hotel and all these meals in restaurants.

"Now"—and he stabbed his finger at me after each word, for emphasis—"don't . . . you . . . EVER . . . act that way again!"

My mom was more hesitant. She could see I was slacking off in my work habits, trying to get away with doing less and less, but she was afraid anything she said would only make it worse. I was really taking it easy at practice. I went every day, like I always had, six days a week, four hours a day, mornings and afternoons. I even won races. But I wasn't pushing myself. I wasn't trying to better my times, I wasn't trying to toughen up mentally, I wasn't paying attention to the coach, and I wasn't really focused on any goal. My mother knew it; my coach knew it. They just didn't know what to do about it.

Then one day a psychiatrist relative of my stepdad's who was staying with us from out of town asked me to explain why I spent all those hours doing lap after lap, missing out on downtime with my friends. "It's gotta be so boring, going up and down the lane," he said. "Why do you do it? Why do you keep swimming?"

And my mother overheard me answer, "Um, I dunno."

Well. She took me back into my room and sat me down and let all the pent-up worry and fear and frustration pour out.

"Summer, if you really don't know why you're swimming, then we've got to talk," I remember her saying. "You know, you don't have to do this. *Don't* do this, unless it's for yourself. You don't have to please me, or your dad, or your coach, or anybody else. I have a lot of other things I could do with my time than take you to practice at five in the morning. And I could use the money. Four hundred a month is money I don't have to throw around.

"Here's what I don't understand," she continued. "If you're going to give up as much as you are giving up, why wouldn't you want to put everything you've got into it? Why wouldn't you try to be the best you can be?

"You think about it," she told me levelly, "and you make a decision."

She definitely got my attention.

I started listening to my coach instead of trying so hard to work in a wisecrack during his lectures so the older kids would laugh and think I was cool. And I started swimming—really going all out, so that I didn't just win, I improved my times. My coach had been right: attitude, not ability, was keeping me from getting faster.

But it wasn't that my mom had set me on a new course: she'd put me back on my own, by reminding me of what I'd done and what I still wanted to do. It was still my dream, and she wouldn't take ownership, not even for a minute, not even if I dropped it in her lap or insisted she pick it up for me. If I were to say, "I really don't feel like going to practice today," trying to force her to force me, she'd just turn the decision back on me. "Do you think that's a good idea?" she'd ask, or "Is there a reason why you don't want to go?"

I couldn't make her assume responsibility for my choices. If I wanted to quit, or throw away my talent by slacking off, that was my prerogative. But she wouldn't let me pretend that I wasn't responsible, that somehow I wasn't to blame later. She'd make sure I was made perfectly aware of my own accountability.

My mother never lost sight of her job as a parent, not even that awful year she insisted she didn't know how to parent. Her concern was the adult I was growing up to be, not the star athlete I might become. She called me to the carpet not about my athletic performance but about my attitude and personal behavior. It was simply unacceptable. "Swim or don't swim," she told me, "but if you swim—give it your best. Otherwise, what's the point?"

Being There as Parents

Our parents—mine, and those of my Olympic friends—were focused on who we were, not on what we could do. They never lost that focus, never lost sight of their responsibility as parents, even when our athletic success might have blinded them to the people we were becoming. Our parents were interested in sport as a character-forming experience, not as an index of self-worth. For our parents, the Olympics were just another leg in our journey; the Games were never a destination beyond which nothing mattered. What was important to them was how we played the game, not whether or not we won. What was important was that we were givers, not takers—that we gave our best in whatever we did, and that ultimately we gave of ourselves in such a way that we left the world a better place than we found it.

And what was important to us was knowing our parents were being *parents,* paying close attention to who we were as people, ready to catch us if we fell, applaud us if we didn't, and keep us centered and sane no matter how wild the circus around us became. That's what got us all the way to the Olympics and then up to that topmost platform.

"My greatest moment," Dot confirms, "was standing up there, after they hung that gold medal around my neck, and seeing my parents and Marge Ricker, my first coach—straight in front of me. That Olympic podium could have been positioned anywhere in the stadium, but it happened to be placed so that when I stood up, there they were: the people I most wanted to share that particular second with. It was one of the most beautiful moments of the Olympics. 'THANK YOU!' I yelled. Then I raised my arms. 'I LOVE YOU,' I said.

"I wished they could hear me," Dot says with a sigh. "But it didn't matter. They knew."

4

The Third Parent:
What Makes a Coach Great

Parents are always asking me what makes a coach great. They ask this because they want to know how to go about finding one for their kid. Or if their kid already has one, they want to know if they should leave well enough alone. They're not sure what kind of coach/athlete relationship is the best for their child. They're not sure how to spot a bad coach when they see one, and then they're not sure what to do about it when they do. Parents want to know when to sit by, when to step in, and what to say and do once they decide to take action.

I'll say this at the outset: growing up, my own experience with coaches did not require much in the way of intervention from my parents. I never found myself in a situation from which I needed to be saved. My parents never felt any need to chase after a winning team or coach who might get me up the competitive ladder faster. I stayed with the coaches I wound up with by staying on the same club team from the age of six until I was seventeen.

Ralph Thomas, my first coach, was just fine—although I'm not sure all parents today would think so. He didn't attempt to make us into serious swimmers. Ralph couldn't see what girls under the age of ten had to gain by being subjected to two-hour, gnarly, all-out practices. He didn't even believe we should show up every afternoon. "Let 'em have fun," he advised our parents. Ralph wanted us to have a good time, mainly, and to feel, bit by bit, the measure of our success.

Not every parent agreed with his laid-back approach. My own mother tells me she fretted a lot about whether or not to put me into more intensive programs. "You were doing so well, you could have probably done a lot better," she recalls. But she did her homework; she knew a lot of coaches from hanging around the pool scene as our mom and as a volunteer and assistant. She talked to them as well as to other coaches they suggested about her concerns. And they all said the same thing: "If you put her in a really strenuous regimen now, you're going to lose her when it really matters."

That advice made sense to my mom. She put her fears aside, regardless of what the other parents thought or did. My friend Stephanie's parents, for example, thought nothing of switching her from team to team, coach to coach. But my mom was never one to bow to peer pressure. She was more concerned about the smile on my face, the joy I took in my sport. I went to swim practice because I had fun with my friends, not because I was intent on being the youngest star to ever leap off the blocks. For her to yank me off my team in pursuit of some goal *she* prized— well, she wouldn't do it.

"I had this intuitive feeling that you were something special," my mom explains, "and that I had to do everything I could to allow you to develop your abilities at your own rate. Swimming had to remain your choice, not mine."

When I was ten, my club, SIAC, went through some growing pains that ultimately were resolved by merging with another club to form California Capital Aquatics. As a larger club, we could afford to hire a top-notch coach, and after a few months of trying out candidates, our parents picked Mike Hastings for the job. Mike was a professional: he'd coached John Naber, an Olympic champion, and the Egyptian national team, plus he had years of experience coaching in the Bay Area. Our parents felt lucky to get him, because by this point the idea that swimming might take us places—to college on scholarship, if not to the Olympics—was certainly motivating them to hire someone who could get us to give our best. Mike was my coach from the age of ten until the day I left for Stanford. I even came home from college for the summer so I could train with him.

Mike did his job well. I got into Stanford on a full athletic scholarship to be a member of Richard Quick's celebrated team. In 1990, Richard was arguably the best women's swim coach in the nation, with athletes like Janet Evans and Betsy Mitchell to his credit. Not only did I go to the Olympics with him, but I also spent two of the best swimming years of my life on his team. I think I swam better during the two NCAA championships at Stanford than during the '92 Games in Barcelona. He remained my coach after the Olympics, during my junior year, even though I'd forfeited my place on his team by accepting endorsement jobs and sponsor roles.

That pretty much describes my entire career prior to my ten-month comeback in 1995. Aside from summer rec and high-school swimming, I was a member of only two teams, SIAC/CCA and Stanford, and I had only three head coaches.

You could say I just lucked out. I wouldn't argue. But my parents never trusted in luck to keep me happy and motivated. They were watching out for me the whole time, ready to interfere at the first sign I was miserable, fearful, or lacking inspiration.

My mom was particularly watchful for anybody who was insensitive enough to break my spirit. She was crystal clear on what made a coach great: good chemistry with me. If I'd been unwilling to go to practice, prone to crying fits and tantrums, extra fearful of failure, extra obsessed with winning, she would have noticed, and she would not have stood by silently—more on that in a minute. My being on a winning team, my holding age-group records, my garnering headlines, or my having a coach that was always in the spotlight was never the priority, never what gave her peace of mind. It was entirely a matter of my well-being, a topic on which she was an expert. The question she asked herself continually was, Did I take joy in my sport? If so, then everything else would take care of itself. A coach who kept me passionate was a coach who was doing his job and who required no outside interference or input from any parent.

That's not to imply, however, that my coaches were all nice guys who didn't ask much or push hard. On the contrary, like my mom, they understood that asking for my very best—expecting nothing less, accepting nothing less—was a way of showing how much they cared. And by asking the very best of themselves, they inspired me, by example, to give mine.

Great coaches, like great parents, don't have to demand or threaten; they inspire things like hard work, persistence, commitment, passion, drive, and goal-mindedness by living those traits themselves, day in and day out. They're not in it for the power trip; they're authoritative, not authoritarian. They don't push you to make *their* choices, to fulfill *their* need; they put the responsibility of making choices on you, confident you'll choose well because they're confident they've set the best example possible all along. They *do* ask that you do the work and push the envelope of your talent, because talent is never enough. And because they've earned your respect, you do the work. Willingly. Even *passionately*.

What makes a coach great is simply that: he gets you to work hard enough to prove your talent to yourself, and there's nothing like a glimpse of your own enormous capability to get you psyched. Take a bunch of athletes who deep down believe in their own ability, give them a coach who inspires their diligence until they see that ability shine, and you've got a winning team. That's the formula. It's true for coaching; it's true, too, for parenting.

My friends agree. Karch Kiraly's first great coach was new to the job, but his philosophy was totally field-tested; he'd been a player Karch and his dad competed against in beach tournaments, and he believed in hard conditioning. So months before the team was to assemble for practice, he called them together and asked that they pair off in training duos and devote their preseason to getting in super shape doing "stadiums." Karch remembers those fall afternoons in their small football arena. He and a teammate would run up the ten concrete stadium steps twenty times. Then they'd jump up the ten steps twenty times. They they'd jump up twenty times in two-footed hops. Then they'd hop up twenty times on their left foot, then on their right foot, and finally, up two, down one. By the end of the workout, they had each jumped maybe a thousand times up those concrete bleachers. The whole team did it. "We were diligent," Karch says. "Our attitude was 'Let's do what our coach wants, because we want to see what we can do.' "

For the first time, his team made the state championships. They lost in the finals, but never before had they come so far. After that season, Karch entered his first Open beach tournament and made it to the final day of play, all the way to ninth place out of sixty-four.

"We thought we had some great talent," Karch explains, "but until our coach got us to work that hard, we'd never gone that far in a state tournament."

My first great coach, Mike Hastings, lived by the same equation: If you did the work, in and out of the pool, you'd get results. If you didn't come to practice, if you slacked off/on in the weight room, there was no gimmick or miracle in the world that was going to get you to the wall first in competition.

Mike earned our respect by making us earn his. He wouldn't put up with crap from anybody from day one. I'll never forget him blasting me for being late that very first day; it wasn't my fault, as my mother made perfectly clear, but for all he knew, my showing up fifteen minutes late was a pattern he needed to nip in the bud. There were, in fact, some guys on our team who were used to getting away with murder. Right before Mike signed on we briefly had a coach named Charlie who simply could not get certain swimmers into the pool. They'd hang out in the locker room for the entire practice and he'd let them, not because he was a terrible coach but because he was still green enough to think that he needed to be Mr. Nice Guy all the time. But when these same guys tried to pull that stunt with Mike, waltzing out onto the pool deck after the rest of us had started our practice sets, Mike said, "What do you think you're doing? You're way too late for practice. Get dressed and go home."

He also wouldn't tolerate any of us talking while he was talking; he couldn't stand it when we didn't pay close attention. Guys like Bill Hickman, who would do anything for a laugh, really got on Mike's nerves. Bill would crack a joke in lane eight while Mike was talking in lane one, and suddenly, you'd see Mike take off his glasses, hold them at his hip, and stare at Bill until Bill shut up. "IF YOU THINK I'M GONNA STAND UP HERE AND WASTE MY TIME WHILE YOU GOOF OFF . . . ," he'd start in on Bill. Or Bill would fail to streamline when he pushed off, even though Mike had just reminded him to. Mike would pull him out of the water and make him hold the streamlined position, freezing his butt off, for maybe ten minutes.

Mike would yell at Bill, but that was because he really cared about him. Mike would just *ignore* complete goof-offs. He would tolerate no interference, no interruptions to our two-hour practices. Not even lightning necessarily canceled our workouts. We'd see the sky flash and think, "No practice today *for sure*." But Mike was a meteorologist. He knew when lightning was a real threat, and when it wasn't—and nineteen out of twenty times, it wasn't. "That's just sheet lightning," he'd say. "Get back in the pool." We weren't always so sure; one time we were all a little worried, so we yelled to Walter, who wore braces, "IT'S GONNA GET YOU FIRST!" That rattled him so bad, he got out and went home. But you couldn't scare Mike: he knew his weather. If he did let us get out, more often than not we'd just wait out the storm and get right back in to finish our workout.

One practice, Mike almost made me cry. I was probably twelve. I hadn't come to practice the day before because it had poured rain (remember, most pools in California are outside). Rain wasn't a very good reason to stay home—I probably just didn't feel like coming. So when I walked out onto the pool deck, Mike said, "Where were you yesterday?"

"Well," I said, "it was raining."

He got this sarcastic look on his face. "Oh—it was *raining*? Like you were going to get *more* wet while you're swimming?"

I knew it was an idiotic reason. A baby excuse. His sarcasm stung me so badly, I never wanted to upset him again.

"I did have a fear Mike would crush you," my mother admits. "That's why I set him straight that first day. I told him to be really careful, that you were really sensitive."

But aside from that one sarcastic outburst, Mike *was* really careful. He got my number right away. He was a good judge of people; what worked with some might not be the best tactic with others. When I blew a race, he understood I already felt terrible; he never talked down at me, he never yelled at me, he simply asked, "Well, where do you think you went wrong?" Whereas with other people—Bill, for instance—Mike hounded them. He knew Bill could take it; he understood Bill needed it. And he didn't set out to crush Bill's comedic role, because he understood Bill contributed something to our team that couldn't be measured on a clock. There were times when we'd all be laughing so hard at something Bill had done or said, we'd have to hold on to the wall so we wouldn't drown. Then it was all Mike could do not to crack up, too. "I can't be-*lieve* you," Mike would say to Bill, his face all twisted with the effort of trying to stay solemn.

What was evident to both my parents was that this coach really poured his energy and devotion into those of us who were giving it our all. Mike tried to appear evenhanded, but you pretty much got from him what you gave him. Like my mom, he decided the fairest way to allocate his attention was simply to match his level of commitment to the swimmer's. There were always kids who'd complain about his not noticing them, not participating in their workout; it wasn't true—he'd cheer anybody who was having an awesome practice. But he wasn't fooled by the occasional performer. He'd ask, "Who went and did weights?" and you couldn't lie; if you weren't pumping iron outside of practice, he'd know, because it would show in your workout, just as it would show if you *were* making that kind of extra effort. He wanted us to know that we were fooling only ourselves if we thought we were fooling him. Those of us who put in the work got Mike to put the work into us.

I was especially intent on getting Mike's attention, because after that blowout on day one, I felt I had to prove myself to him. Most of us did; our coach had been around greatness, his experience was written all over him, and we didn't want to let him down. We wanted his respect, because it really counted for something. Since nothing motivated me more than getting what wasn't given readily, I set out to really impress him.

I'll never forget one afternoon after I'd swum ten 100 IMs as though I were in a real race and not just some weekday practice session. He came over and said, "We should look at putting you in the senior group." I'll never forget how he used to pace along the side of the pool, keeping up with me—maybe we'd be doing ten 200s, each one faster than the last, and during the last three, I'd see Mike jumping up and down, he was so excited at my times. There was simply no better feeling in the world than seeing him get so emotional, simply because you really had to earn his enthusiasm. I fed off it. It made me feel like we were working as a team, like we were really in this together.

Mike understood that nothing drove me harder than the suggestion that something I wanted was out of my reach. So in practice as well as competition, he'd say to me, "You probably won't be able to do this, but . . ." It worked every time: *Oh yeah? Wanna bet?* was my automatic competitor's response. And Mike knew just how to defuse the expectation bomb that was ticking inside me before a race. Before the '88 Olympic Trials, I remember him saying, "Now, Summer, look at it as just another meet. Just use it for the experience." It was his way of saying, "Winning would be great, but it's your all-out effort that counts most." It accomplished the same thing my parents did; it reminded me that winning wasn't the definition of my self-worth: they loved me regardless. Swimming was only part of a much larger picture: I had a life—a full life—outside of swimming, and giving my all was all anyone could ask.

In fact, Mike operated on the same principle my parents did: he treated me with trust and respect. If he asked me to give a little extra, it was in the form of a challenge, never a command. "You probably can't do this many sets in this time . . ." was a typical Mike sort of phrasing. Or he'd say, "Let's see what we can do," as though it weren't me alone out there but us as a team, working together. He never spoke with the attitude "You'll listen to me because I'm God"; he never pretended he had all the answers. He never belittled me to affirm his own authority, never said, "Don't tell me how to coach—you're fourteen, what do you know?" Mike respected my experience as well as my ability; after all, I'd been swimming for years. So he'd ask me how I felt, and he'd listen intently to my answer—out of sincere respect and interest.

In short, Mike put me in the driver's seat. Like my parents, he made it clear that how far and how fast I went depended entirely on me, on how much work I was willing to put into it. And like my parents, he also assured me he'd sit right next to me until I felt secure enough to drive all by myself. He taught me to analyze my own performance—what I was doing right as well as what I was doing wrong—so that I'd internalize his coaching until I no longer needed it, or felt secure without it. Like good parenting, the object of good coaching, as Mike saw it, was to give a kid enough self-knowledge through hard work that she could make choices for herself, choices informed by her own experience. If he did his job right, I'd reach a point where I could coach myself. He believed good coaches succeed when they work themselves out of a job. My mom and dad believed the same was true of good parents.

Mike trained me to know my stroke and body so well, I could figure out my time at the end of a sprint nearly to the second. It was our little game: He'd ask me, at the wall, "So whaddya think you did?" and it was uncanny, I almost always guessed the exact time. And in competition, if I didn't swim well, Mike wouldn't rush up and tell me where and how: he'd ask me to evaluate myself first. That had a way of diffusing my anger and tears, too: by the time I'd told him what went wrong, he could say, "Mmm. You weren't aggressive enough on your turns . . ." or "The dive *was* terrible," and get both of us laughing.

He wanted me to feel I knew even more than he did about my performance, because he understood that would serve me better when I couldn't have him around—like when I was up on the blocks at a major event like the World Championships, or the Goodwill Games. He didn't want me to think of him as the only one who could get me to win. He wanted me to know how to make my own decisions about how to warm up, how to mentally prepare, and how to squeeze the most out of any competitive window that might open up during a race.

I came to see how critical that was, how *empowering*, when I went on National team trips. My big rival when I was fifteen, sixteen, and seventeen was a girl named Mary Ellen. Mary Ellen's coach ruled her life. My friends and I called him Little Napoleon. He'd write out every detail of every workout for every day of the meet, and she seemed to believe that if she didn't follow his orders to the letter, she couldn't possibly win. One morning, she showed up at the pool without her workout, having left it in her room, and she fell apart. She almost didn't get in the water, because she hadn't the first clue about what to do. You could see her up there, debating whether to go back to her room (the hotel was a twenty-minute drive away) and get the workout. She finally got in the water, and we all helped her. But she still wasn't convinced that what she did was right.

That was in 1990, a year after she had broken American records, a year after *Sports Illustrated* featured her as the Up-and-Comer breaststroker. The following year, at the 1991 World

Championships, she lost it. I've always suspected it was because her coach abused the control he had over her. She went on to a different coach, but it was too late; she never quite got back what had apparently been taken from her.

WHILE I NEVER had the experience of working with them, I saw plenty of coaches who extorted results by using fear, coaches who bullied their team members into giving what they weren't ready to give willingly, and coaches who were control freaks or powermongers.

There were a couple of isolated instances where my teammates and I shrank in horror at what some other team's coach would say or do. We saw one coach walk up to one of his swimmers, a girl with beautiful long hair, and after she had gotten out of the pool he demanded, "You go cut off your hair. Now." We were inches away, my friends and I, from going up to him and saying, "What the hell are you doing?" But the girl did it.

I remember two coaches in particular who were over the edge. One coach couldn't get through a meet without making someone on his team cry. During warm-ups, he'd make his girls, these itty-bitty girls, swim with panty hose on, tennis shoes on—anything to make what was already hard even harder. At meets he'd be dodging in and out, waving this sheet of paper with heat times at them in the pool, or walking really fast along the lane, holding the stopwatch up high, his arm stiff. He'd yell nonstop, and while I never heard what he said, he was so in-their-face that somebody would be bawling. Tears after losing a race aren't all that unusual, but these girls were much more affected than that; they were terrified.

The other coach I'll never get out of my mind managed to instill such fear in his swimmers that they'd literally hide from him after a race if they hadn't done well. I'd try to talk to one of them, and she'd say, "Can't-talk-gotta-go" and run off to disappear in the crowd. He'd track the girl down, give her this evil look, and then, with his finger stabbing home every point, he'd say, "That was AWFUL! I can't BELIEVE you blew that! That's the WORST I've ever seen you swim! You could have done SO much better!" Never once did the girl's expression change; whatever joy she might have ever had for her sport had long since been stamped out of her. He'd demand she and her teammates get in the warm-up pool and, instead of doing 1,000 yards, make them do 2,000—as punishment. As far as he was concerned, there was nothing good to comment on, let alone reward, short of absolute perfection.

In my mind, this sort of coach is as damaging as those parents who push, push, push because they're too afraid they won't get what they want out of their children any other way. And this sort of coach is just as ineffective as that sort of parent: I have yet to hear of an athlete who had a terrible power-struggle relationship with his or her coach go on to win Olympic gold medals, or become the top seed, or otherwise command the field. I don't know of any truly successful children of control-freak parents, either. To be sure, lots of talented athletes go very far, surprisingly far, despite a troubled coach or parent relationship. But they don't go all the way. Sooner or later, the chemistry of the relationship poisons the effort.

Take Debi Thomas, the skater who won the bronze medal in Calgary in 1988. From the start of her formal training at the age of twelve, the relationship with her coach, Alex McGowan, was a rocky one. "I was brought up to express my opinion," Debi explains. "He was a British dictator. I'd state my opinion and I'd get into trouble."

The big divide was a philosophical one. McGowan insisted Debi needed to practice more and focus on school less in order to be a world champion. Debi insisted on doing both; since she'd been five, she had wanted to become a doctor. His response: "Why be a doctor when you can make all this money in Ice Capades?"

"Even as a child, I can remember going through these ridiculous discussions," says Debi. "Mr. McGowan would say, 'I need you in here for more ice time.' I'd say, 'I gotta study.' My mom would tell him, 'She has tests, she has her future, and frankly, that's more important. You'll get her when you can get her.' My mom basically put it on the line."

Debi threatened to quit every week. "It got so my coach would taunt that they were going to have a party for me every time I'd make this threat," she says. "I loved to skate; I just needed a break. My mom sure didn't push me—she'd let me vent, let me rampage, do what she could to do what my coach wanted but also protect me. I didn't want to skate on Saturday mornings, because I'm not a morning person. I wanted to be home, eating sugary cereal, watching cartoons. I thought Saturday-morning practice was a waste of time, so I'd show up half an hour late, an hour late, and go to the end of the rink to work on my figures. 'What are you doing!' Mr. McGowan would scream. 'Put your freestyle skates on!' I'd do my program and miss the first three things. I'd start throwing a raging fit, and he'd threaten to have me thrown out of the rink.

"Finally," Debi continues, "I said, 'Can we save a few steps and not have me come in on Saturday?' He felt if I missed an hour, I'd be an hour worse, but I thought I was an hour worse off by training badly. I don't know what my mom said, but she must have said something, because I do know I stopped going on Saturdays."

But as Debi got older, her mom couldn't run interference, and the power struggle intensified. Debi barely made it to Calgary with her coach relationship intact; she threatened to compete coachless. Things came to a head after the opening ceremonies: Debi wanted to relax after practices and enjoy the Olympics, but Mr. McGowan had gotten her extra ice time several hours away from the Olympic training facility. Every hour she didn't train, he reminded her, she'd be one hour worse. When Debi resisted, he threatened to have her boyfriend, Brian, sent home.

"I felt like I was in a prison," Debi recalls. "Even though I was twenty, I wasn't strong enough to fight for what I knew was right for me. My mom couldn't help me; she couldn't get to me in the Village. So I said fine, I'll do the extra ice time. It was at the expense of being at the Olympics. I'll regret that the rest of my life—that I didn't enjoy my one chance to be part of that experience."

She spent every hour of her Olympic stay practicing, practicing, practicing. By the time she got out on the ice for the event the world awaited—a final showdown with Katarina Witt—she was totally burned out. "I felt like a zombie," says Debi. "Not even adrenaline was going through me.

"Maybe if I'd taken in the Olympic experience differently—you know, enjoyed the Jamaican bobsled team, watched the ski jumping—I would have realized I was there, at the OLYMPICS! But instead, it felt like any old competition to me. So while I waited for the music to start, I said to myself, 'Maybe my body will automatically do it'—which I've never believed in my life."

On the first jump combination she landed on two feet and Debi thought, *There goes the program of your life.* By the time she hit the triple loop and her hand went down, she was thinking, *If I get off the ice right now, how bad would it look?*

"For me to do that in the most important competition of my life," Debi continues, "I say, every day, *'What were you thinking? You needed to make that moment happen!'* "

What haunts her to this day is not the fact that her medal is bronze instead of gold; what haunts her is knowing that she didn't go out and do her best, for which she blames herself. It was her moment, she says, her show—and she blew it. She does not blame her coach. She's adamant that no one else blame her coach.

And maybe it's not my place to blame her coach. But I can't help but think that Debi's career and her performance at Calgary prove my point: good chemistry between coach and athlete is more important than anything, no matter how gifted the coach, how excellent his technique, how many other stars he's turned out, how much training or what kind of training he insists on, how much of a media darling he is, how respected he is in the field.

Debi doesn't think she had much choice as far as a coach was concerned. Alex McGowan was one of the best in the state, the kind of star coach a skater with any promise would be honored to have. Technically, he was unmatched. "He knew how things needed to be done to be absolutely correct, and when you're twelve, that's what you need," says Debi. There was only one other coach in the area with McGowan's level of expertise, and Debi opted not to train with her.

And she stuck with him, even when she knew intuitively that all the fighting couldn't be worth it. In Colorado, at the U.S. training facility, Debi went to talk to other coaches about taking her on. "I was this close to switching—during the competitive season, right before a major event!" says Debi. "In fact, I was ready to go forward as the favorite of this country, with no coach at all! That's how far it got." But her agent advised against it, and in truth, Debi wasn't sure ditching McGowan would have had any happier an outcome.

"You have to understand," she explains, "that it's very difficult to leave a coach you've been with ten years and won championships with. I could have left and *still* ended up being a disaster. And then, the rest of my life, I'd get 'I told you so.' "

When parents ask me what to do about a star coach who's nevertheless spatting with their child—verbally, emotionally or psychologically—I urge them to find someone else. If the relationship isn't a positive one, nothing positive can ultimately come from it.

As I've said, my mom didn't have to shop around for a coach for me. She felt on the whole that Mike Hastings, despite his temper flares and sarcastic outbursts, had all the right stuff as far as working with me was concerned. Mike shared her insistence on instilling personal responsibility: allowing for my mistakes and their consequences, giving a lot of rein but never being indulgent, and never threatening but always being consistent in follow-through. As I've said, Mike would never allow us to kid ourselves or others about whom was to blame for a failure: If we didn't reach our goals, the blame rested with no one but ourselves. Likewise, if we were to win or exceed our goals, the victory was totally ours, and totally satisfying.

My mother will tell you she was terribly grateful the year I was fourteen, that I had someone like Mike to look up to and listen to, because I was a total jerk. I'd show up for practice but swim mechanically, I'd joke around with everybody on the pool deck instead of listening to Mike, I'd whine about my times but not make any real effort to improve them. It was Mike who said, "You think you're working hard, but look at it, be honest with yourself: Are you really putting everything you have into it? And if not, *why come at all?*" My mom had said pretty much the same thing, but Mike got through to me in a way she could not.

The one or two times Mike overstepped his place, however, my mom was the one to get through to him—not to tell him how to do his job, but rather, to show him she knew hers. She never questioned his coaching decisions with comments like "Why is Summer in this event?" or "Why have her practice butterfly?" even though she had enough knowledge in the sport to do so. She just reminded him that, as a mother, she was an authority on her own child. *I'd like to let you know a little bit about Summer* was her tactic. She would never have said, "Where do you get off talking to my daughter like that?" But she did say to Mike, quietly but forcefully, the day he started as our coach and blasted me for being late, "You will not talk to Summer like that, because she's very sensitive." It was totally clear in her mind that this was her job as my parent. She might have guessed what I needed as a swimmer, but she absolutely *knew* what I needed as her daughter.

Likewise, my dad never presumed to tell Mike how to do his job—but my dad wouldn't allow Mike to tell him his, either. The infamous year I turned fourteen, my dad decided what I needed was not to swim harder or be more dedicated and focused, but to take a breather. That was one hundred and eighty degrees from what my mother and Mike thought was good for me. But my dad was convinced, and he acted on his conviction. He came in and told Mike, "I'm taking Summer for a week's vacation."

"But, Bob," my coach said, "this would be the worst time for her to go away! It's January, right in the heart of our training for the spring meets! A break now will cost her dearly in competition!"

"You misunderstand me," my dad said. "I'm taking her to Mexico. You say which week."

I went with my brother and dad to Club Med for an entire week, during which I did not once work out doing laps. When I came back, I had the best season of my career. (After that, in fact, Mike used to ask my dad, "When are you taking Summer on vacation?")

My dad was never fuzzy on what his role should be. He told Mike once, "I won't interfere with your decisions as Summer's coach if you won't interfere with mine as her father."

On the whole, I think what made Mike so great was that he didn't feel the need to compete with my parents; he valued their role and respected their input, different, occasionally, as it was. He recognized that my mom knew me in a way he could not— all my innermost fears and desires—and he was a good enough

coach to take advantage of her insights. Very early in our relationship, when I was maybe eleven or twelve, my mom had
Mike over to dinner and we talked about how incredible it
would be if I were to go to the Olympics someday. I brought it
up, not them. After I'd gone to bed, Mike said to my mom,
"You know, shooting for the Olympics is a very big deal, and
most kids don't make it." My mom said, "Mike, you don't
know Summer very well, so let me tell you: *If she decides this is
something she wants to do, she will.* You can put money on it."

The key to Mike's greatness as a coach was respect. He respected me as an authority on my own ability and potential,
and he respected my parents as an authority on me. My parents
respected him as an authority on my swimming, and I respected
Mike because he asked and expected what my parents asked and
expected of me: to set goals for myself, and put in whatever
work was required to meet them.

IF THIS HADN'T been the case—if Mike didn't know his job,
didn't take a supportive tack with me, didn't listen to my parents—one or both of my parents would have most certainly
taken the steps necessary to get me another coach. "If you were
disgruntled with Mike," my mom tells me now, "and had said,
in so many words or gestures, 'Mom, I cannot swim for this
man, I have to go someplace else,' I would have helped you do
that, even if it had meant we moved, even if it meant you went
and lived with another family."

Sadly, a lot of parents I grew up with didn't fully understand
this as their responsibility. Mary Ellen would probably have
been better off had she been made to understand that she was

fragile. No parent seemed to blow the whistle on the maniac coach who made his girls swim with tennis shoes and scared his entire team into crying fits. I'm not sure why. Surely a parent who pays close attention can recognize the difference between a child who cares about doing well and a child who is utterly obsessed with her performance, a child who's upset after blowing a race and one who's totally terrified to lose. Temper tantrums, running and hiding from a coach, and even dead silence about practice are all red flags that something is wrong. I'm not saying that tough talk and iron discipline are the hallmarks of an abusive coach. It's when the negatives outweigh anything positive and the child's scared to death to go to practice and equally scared to quit that a parent might seriously consider switching coaches or teams.

My mom didn't have to be shown any red flags: she made a practice of going to practice just to be sure she missed nothing that she would have felt obliged to act on. And by sticking around, talking to coaches and other parents, watching other teams in action, asking questions and getting answers, she kept herself in the loop so that if she did have to save me from some awful coach, she was armed with the knowledge to act swiftly. She did her homework. She knew the sport, the competition, and the program. She saw that as part of her job.

In the end, I knew Mike had my mom's vote of confidence if only because getting me to his practices required superhuman dedication of her. For four years, our club was without a consistent pool facility: we swam all over the Fair Oaks region, in L-shaped pools, in pools without lane lines, in country club pools, in pools where there were no flags to warn you in the backstroke that you were about to hit the wall. And as hard as it may have been on us swimmers, it was even harder on our parents, to shuttle us all over the county. When I turned fourteen, CCA worked out an arrangement with a Jesuit school in Sacramento whose pool facility was incredible. But that pool was a good forty-five-minute drive from Roseville, and for my mom, who had to hold a job, getting me to and from there twice a day was a real hurdle. It wasn't easy to stay committed to my club, and if she hadn't thought the world of Mike, she wouldn't have.

"I Expect This"

Mike was my coach for about eight years, long enough for me to miss seeing his satisfaction when I swam in college. I'd call him up, even while I was training with Richard Quick, and say, "These were my times, were they good?"

Richard had a very different style. He didn't ever say, "You probably won't be able to do ten fifties under this amount of time, but give it your best. . . ." No. Richard would say, "Okay: Ten fifties in this time."

He didn't hope we could do it; he *expected* us to do it. Period.

Everybody's response to these declarations was typically, "No way! We can't do that! You're nuts!" I took them as a challenge, though. *Can I do it,* I wondered, *because he expects it?*

The only way this strategy could possibly work was for Richard to absolutely know what we could do out there, and he did know, because he had the experience. He was totally certain of our potential—and so we came to fulfill his expectations. When Richard spoke, there were no "ums" or "ahs" or pauses of any kind: it was the voice of Total Conviction. "Here's what you need to do, here's the time you need, and you can do it," he'd say, not like he was selling the idea to us, but as though he was stating unequivocal facts (not unlike my mother insisting, "Summer, you can do anything you put your mind to"). Richard got us to believe we could do anything by having us prove it to ourselves, over and over. He'd force us to set our own goals high, and then remind us at every opportunity that we had accomplished the outrageous. "See?" he'd say. "See how fast you can go?"

During those last races in Barcelona, I came to appreciate his tactic. Right before my gold-medal race, Richard stepped up to me and said in that emphatic no-ifs-ands-or-buts way he had, "Nobody in the world can swim butterfly faster, longer than you can. *You own this race.*" It wasn't a challenge, it wasn't a prayer, it wasn't a last-ditch gimmick; it was a reminder of a fact he had made me establish for myself. It had the same effect as when, years before, a friend of my mom's had come up to me right before I was to race against Corey Saxon, whose backstroke time was better than mine, and said: "You can beat her! She can't be that much faster than you; she's in the next lane!" History will show I responded really well to this kind of affirmation.

In personality and temperament, Richard was nothing like Mike. Whereas Mike was moody, Richard was irrepressibly sunny. Each morning we'd meet at 5:30 in the guard office next to the pool, and there was Richard with his huge plastic mug of an awful swill called Sport Tea, singing little country-western ditties and dancing. "How ya doin', Summer!" he'd greet me in this funny voice, and then he'd laugh this *hee-hee-hee* laugh. "Had my Sport Tea!" he'd add, as if he had to explain why he had way too much energy for a normal person at 5:30 A.M. We used to kid him about that tea—too much ginseng, we figured. "Man, Richard," we'd say, "look what it's doin' to you! You gotta knock off that stuff." Then we'd put on our caps and hope that for once—just once!—the guys' team would precede us out of the warm and bright guard room into the dark and cold pool area, but *noooo*. Richard couldn't wait. "Let's go swimmin', women!" he'd say, and out we'd go. We'd plunge into the water, steam rising into the predawn blackness, and Richard would prance alongside us. "G-g-gooooo!" he'd yell, unable to contain his enthusiasm.

And while the slightest lapse in our attention would send Mike Hastings flying off the handle, Richard Quick very rarely spoke sharply. I can honestly remember only one incident. "STOP COMPLAINING OR GET OUT!" he yelled at one of my teammates, Jenny, who'd just whined one too many times that morning. We all froze—twenty-six girls in a ten-lane pool. The expression on his face, and the forcefulness of how he said it, brought us all to attention.

But like Mike, and like my parents, Richard practiced what he preached; he drove himself as hard as, if not harder than, he drove us. He was always in motion, running to keep in shape. Richard would get down on the floor and do aerobics with us; when he struggled, we couldn't help but kid him: "What, you can't take this?" He had a way of grunting and screaming— "Anh, anh, ahn"—with each leg lift that made us feel embarrassed for him. But the commitment he showed we respected. It inspired our own commitment—both to him and to achieving our common goals.

With Richard, there was no giving less than one hundred percent. He cut himself no slack: even when his bad knees forced him to a hobble, he'd get on his bike to get in a workout. So when I developed a shoulder problem late in my freshman year—a tweaking dull pain that hurt enough to break my concentration—he was determined I get in a workout even if I couldn't swim. He'd have me do an hour's biking on a stand-up bike—you literally stood up to pedal—right there on the pool deck while the rest of the team swam. "Okay, two minutes hard, one minute moderate," he'd say, which for Richard meant two minutes of near-puking, one minute of hard. He'd cheer for me, but watching everybody in the water put me in a foul temper when I had to work out on the bike. For the second hour of practice, he had me put on stubby half-fins called zoomers and swim with my injured arm at my side. I was dead tired from the bike; swimming with the zoomers on my feet blistered them so badly that I had to wear socks while I worked out in them in the water; and swimming with one arm made that arm so tired it started to feel injured.

One afternoon, I just couldn't take it anymore. "ARRGHH! SCREW THIS!" I said, and stomped off into the locker room because I was so near tears.

Richard ran into the women's locker room after me—and for Richard, a straitlaced guy, that was a first. "Summer," he said in this quiet, earnest voice, "I know this sucks. I know this is hard."

Then he told me a story about one of my biggest heroes, Betsy Mitchell. She was one of the toughest swimmers out there—a world-record holder in the backstroke—and Richard

had been her coach. "Betsy had the exact same shoulder problem," he told me, "and she went through the exact same thing
you are: four straight months of just kicking. But right after she
recovered she went to a meet and broke a world record.

"There's good that will come out of this," he added. "Stay
focused."

Richard knew I needed just that little pep talk. I went back
into the pool, did what I could, which wasn't much, and hung
in there.

Meanwhile, I was working with Richard's wife, June, a sports
therapist. I'd go over to their house so June could show me the
exercises and work with me. But summer vacation was looming,
and I wanted to go home to Roseville for the summer and train
with Mike Hastings again. So Richard and June made a videotape for me. Richard demonstrated the exercises I was to do
while June described them.

The injury was awful; I hated it for what it robbed me of,
physically, mentally, and emotionally. But watching Richard on
tape each night was hugely therapeutic. For one thing, he was
funny. Richard thrusting out his chest until his shoulder blades
met, Richard lying across the gymnastics ball—watching him,
my dad and I could not stop laughing, which was the levity I
needed while I did these tedious exercises for my injury. Also,
watching the tape gave me and my dad a little ritual each night:
me doing the exercises, and my father making irreverent cracks
about Richard *Slow,* which is how he always referred to Richard
Quick. I did get better. I did go on to the Olympics a year later.
I'll never know if it was the exercises, or the therapeutic value of
watching those tapes with my dad, or the realization that this
coach of mine was so dedicated to my recovery, so committed

to seeing me fulfill my potential, that I could not possibly let him down.

The Moment of Truth

The following summer, I was in Barcelona for the Games. By some incredible good fortune, both Richard Quick and Mike Hastings wound up coaching our team. Officially Richard was my coach, but Mike had accumulated enough points from having successful swimmers to have been appointed after the Olympic Trials as our team head.

Having both of them there was actually kind of awkward for me. They'd been so key to my success in their own unique and very different ways, I didn't want either one of them to feel like second string. I didn't want Mike to think for a minute that I'd forgotten him, or that my loyalties had shifted forever, but Richard was my official coach and had earned his place there as much as I had, and I wasn't about to disappoint him. I wasn't sure how to play the situation, how to show my loyalty to them both equally. It really preyed on my mind.

After I won the bronze, Richard came up and gave me a hug. I don't remember Mike saying much of anything, or stepping forward. After I took the silver medal in the 200 IM—my second event—Richard came up, put his arms around me, and told the cameraman to turn his lens away, because I was so tired and broken down with nervous exhaustion and physical fatigue. I wasn't at all disappointed—that race was one of my best ever—but the accumulated stress of expectations and Olympic competition made me want every bit of support around me, including Mike. And he wasn't there.

Finally it came time for my very last race, the 200 butterfly—my best event. Right before my warm-up, Richard took me aside and said, "I just want to make sure you're focused." *Are you kidding me?* I felt like saying. *I've swum nine races between prelims and finals in the Olympic Games, this is my last race, I couldn't be under more pressure, and you think I'm not focused?!* But instead I dove in, did my warm-up, and pushed all thoughts and emotions about Richard and Mike out of my mind. They were here because I was here. I was here to do a job. I was going out to do it. I thought, *It's my time, it's me on the line, all me.* I got out of the pool, put on my racing suit and sweats, and checked in with the ready room monitor.

Then Richard came up and said what later I heard his wife, June, say he'd never told any other athlete. "Summer," he said, before I was paraded out before the crowds, *"you own this race."*

It was so ironic that, of all the races I was expected to win, I took the gold on that one, because I couldn't have been more tired, emotionally, mentally, and physically. I didn't think I'd be able to finish it. On my third turn, I remember telling myself, *Just finish it, 'cause it'd be too embarrassing if you didn't.* I seriously did not think I was going to get my hands on the wall. I *willed* myself to the end; there was nothing else getting me there.

I touched the wall. I looked back over my shoulder to see the scoreboard.

And then in one fluid motion, screaming at the top of my lungs, I hauled myself out of the water with one arm and, for the first time in my life, shot my other arm, with my elbow locked and my fist closed, as high as I could possibly reach. I can almost see what I must have looked like: head back, mouth wide open, forehead scrunched up like I'm going to cry, only it's more than that, I'm beyond ecstatic, beyond surprised—the whole range of human emotion is there on my face in that one perfect moment.

What I felt most of all, though, was RELIEF. Like a million pounds had been lifted off my shoulders. I'd reached my highest goal. Never mind anybody else's expectations.

Richard was right there. I gave him a big hug when I got out of the pool. Then Mike came down, and I hugged him, and finally, finally, everything was okay. I realized everybody deals with Olympic pressure in different ways; I could imagine a coach thinking he knew this person he'd worked with so many years, or so many hundreds of practices, and yet, in an Olympic situation, you don't want to do the wrong thing, you don't want to say the wrong thing . . . so you say and do nothing, you simply step back and let that athlete do her stuff.

Mike and Richard were, like my parents, two people who loved me and backed me and wanted only the best for me, but who coaxed that best from me in completely different, even opposite, ways. Together with my parents, they made me feel I had a team behind me—a mom, a dad, and a coach each doing the job they did best without ever elbowing in on one another's roles. And separately, they managed to give me exactly what I needed to touch that wall first, not just in my final race for the gold but in every competition I entered, throughout my life, in and out of the pool.

5

The Importance of Mental Toughness:
Cultivating It, Capitalizing on It, Keeping It

Nothing is more dramatic than an athlete taking gold when the stakes are highest or the odds are longest. The most memorable Olympic moments are those defined by a pressure that's almost unbearable to watch, let alone perform under.

The pressure for me to win my final event in Barcelona was off the scale, so far as my audience was concerned. They'd been promised gold in all of my events, and I had delivered only one, in the relay. This was my last opportunity for an individual gold. This was also my best event, the 200 butterfly. It was entirely reasonable for everybody in the world to expect me to win. Or so the press kept reminding them.

My parents sat together in the stands with my aunt. My mom insists she was calm as I mounted the block; "I knew what the outcome would be," she says. My dad kept running between the stands and the bathrooms; his kidneys, like mine, go into overdrive before a competition. He was so excited for me, just for my being there, at the Olympics.

The gun went off. I dove off the starting block.

But I didn't swim the race as I normally did. I didn't get out in front and stay there, dominating all the way, as I always did, as I had just so recently done in Perth for the World Championships. On the last turn for the last lap, I was in third place.

That's when my mom admits she got *very* nervous. "This cannot happen," she remembers thinking. Even my dad knew this wasn't good: "I didn't think you were going to win," he told me later, "because that wasn't your style, to come from behind. You needed to be out in front from the get-go." My mom knew how tired I was, and how my confidence had been deteriorating ever since the 200 medley. She knew, too, I was never good at coming from behind. "I kept thinking," she told me afterward, *" 'She'll be so disappointed if she doesn't win, because knowing her, she'll think she let down America.' "*

When I made my move in that final lap, they were off their seats, screaming. Everybody was. When I touched the wall, they went crazy—my mom with relief, my dad with excitement. "Thank God, thank God," my mother said. My dad still can't talk about it without getting emotional.

I've been a spectator as well, watching athletes pull victory from the jaws of defeat, and there's nothing to match that drama. I remember watching Dan Jansen go into the 1,000 meter in Lillehammer—*what* a nail-biter that was! Everybody watching him knew this was the last race of his career. We all knew he'd been to four Olympics and had yet to nail the gold in the event he won in every other rink in the world. We all knew, by the time he crouched at the starting line, that everything he had worked for, every morning he'd trained in below-zero weather, every injury, every loss, every sacrifice he'd suffered all could be justified or seemingly wasted, depending on how he performed in the next minute or so. It was almost too excruciating to watch—especially when he nicked the boundary line with his skate blade. I remember the commentators saying, "That'll cost him."

Dan not only won the gold, he set a world record in the process.

The hands-down winner, though, when it comes to performing under pressure, is Bonnie Blair. She won her first gold in the 500-meter event in 1988 by beating out an East German skater who had just broken the previous world record. Four years later, with all eyes on her as the defending champion, she won the gold in both the 500- and 1,000-meter events—the first woman ever to take consecutive Winter Olympic golds. And then— when everybody said it simply couldn't be done—she did it again, the following Olympics, in Lillehammer. She won golds in both the 500- and 1,000-meter events. For nine straight years, no one could touch her. No one broke her world record; Bonnie herself broke the record she set in 1988 in the 500. She broke it twice, as a matter of fact, to achieve her personal goal of skating it in under 39 seconds.

We've compared notes, Dan, Bonnie, and I, and we've decided that being able to turn paralyzing pressure into something positive—a competitive edge, even—is what makes a champion out of a natural-born athlete. Seventy percent of the competition is mental, we agree (Debi Thomas insists it's more like 90 percent). If you're not mentally tough, if nerves undo you instead of focus you, if you don't have the inner arrogance that you absolutely have what it takes to win, if you don't see, in your mind's eye, a picture of yourself winning—then you won't win, and not because you can't. You won't succeed in achieving your goals, even if you've got the right coach and natural talent. It doesn't even have to be in athletic competition: succeeding in any arena, at any time in your life, is a matter of mind-set. Mental toughness, inner arrogance, grace under pressure—whatever you want to call it, the winners have it when winning counts the most.

And they're not born with it. Athleticism or ability may be inborn, but the mental edge is definitely something acquired and nurtured.

I credit my own mental toughness to three things: parents who believed, and who nurtured my belief, that I could do whatever I set my heart and mind on doing; parents who valued experience over winning, to the point where they'd let me lose or suffer the consequences of a bad decision; and parents who gave me all the encouragement and support I needed while I was making mistakes so that I could come away with one critical understanding: Failing at something is the best way to learn what it takes to succeed at it.

With that attitude evident in everything they said and did, my parents effectively took the sting out of failure, so that I wouldn't fear it and wouldn't be distracted by it under pressure. Their belief that hard work, experience (including plenty of failure), and a positive mind-set could move mountains meant that I never trusted in talent alone to take me where I wanted to go. And that philosophy—that nothing can take the place of hard work and experience—was what made me a champion, as opposed to one of those thousands of very talented swimmers who somehow never managed to break through.

I've been around enough of those very talented swimmers to know just what I had been given.

When I was training with SIAC in the Fair Oaks region, I got to know this kid Jeremy, who was on the Arden Hills team—where Mark Spitz and Debbie Meyer had gotten their start. Jeremy had probably the most beautiful stroke I've ever seen. He cut through the water effortlessly, like he was a fishline being reeled in. He moved to our team when I was a freshman in high school, and we'd race against each other all the time. He was a natural, the kind of talent who was a surefire bet for the big time.

Over time, though, I came to believe he had a fatal flaw: pressure cracked him like a nut.

He could have had the best workout times of any of us. He could have had the best season of any of us. But as we approached the meet and the mental pressure mounted, Jeremy would start to unravel.

As soon as we started to taper (the precise science of tapering off the intensity of workouts to prepare for competition), he started to overanalyze himself. He took the idea behind taper to a ridiculous extreme. One time his mom said, "Jeremy, could you come stir the pancake batter while I get the griddle?" and he said, "I can't, Mom, because then my arm will get tired, and then it won't match my other arm, and my stroke will be lopsided." Or he'd get to the meet, and during warm-up he'd find some tiny thing slightly off with his stroke. "Oh my gosh—my left arm! It doesn't feel right! I'm not going to swim fast!" And if he didn't have a good sprint before the race in warm-up, he'd be completely thrown. "That's it," he'd say. "I'm doomed."

What held him back from winning an NCAA title later on, I'm convinced, was his mental sabotage. He'd make it all the way to the finals, then fall apart. I'd see him on the blocks, and he wouldn't seem to have that *I'm gonna kick your butt* smile on his face, he didn't have that zoned look of true grit, he didn't radiate that essential sureness in his body language. He looked sick. I could just imagine him wondering, *Should I be jiggling this arm? Should I be splashing water on myself?* He interpreted the smallest thing as some sign of imminent failure. Jeremy lost his races before he ever dove in the water.

Like so many kids who can swim in practice but not in meets, or play the piano with genius but shatter at a recital, Jeremy never figured out how to make experience work for him because, I believe, he wasn't taught to value the experience enough. I can only make guesses, of course, but I suspect Jeremy wasn't taught to rely on himself. Parents who are afraid to let their kids fail often rob them of a variety of experiences, including failure. I think failure is one of the most important experiences in learning how to be successful.

But Jeremy's parents certainly didn't see any inherent good in failure, and so, I suspect, their attitude infected Jeremy. He came to see losing as something out of his control, something, therefore, totally terrifying. He wasn't encouraged enough to embrace it for what it might teach him or to learn, because he'd already been told he had everything it took to make it to the top in the form of sheer talent. Yet, even the kids with the most talent must learn how to bounce back from failure, because it's part of competition. When Jeremy felt that nervous energy building that all athletes feel before competing, he panicked. Nerves simply confirmed for him that he had something to fear, that failure could strike at any moment, due to trivial, random factors. He never hit on the thought sequence or the physical ritual that would give him true inner calm—the kind of calm that silences any voice of doubt, drowns out any buzz of expectation, steadies you, focuses you—because *he* wasn't in control. Because he believed his talent was everything, then he was susceptible to having an "on" day or an "off" day, and he was powerless to change that. So at the slightest suggestion of it being an off day, the voice inside his head whispered, "You're a goner."

And he was.

For most of my career, I didn't fear failure. As unbelievable as that sounds, it's true. My motivation to swim fast was mainly to stay in the running for what became increasingly wonderful opportunities. I had what Justin Huish calls "that backburner attitude"—always saying to myself, *Have fun with it. If it happens, it happens. You're here for the experience.* My parents helped make sure I kept that attitude, by not allowing swimming to consume my life or push everything else to the sidelines: my sport was hardly backburner, but it wasn't ever the whole point of my existence either. And of course, my coaches encouraged the same perspective: Mike Hastings even used those very words, *You're here for the experience.*

Sure I hated to lose; every competitor hates to lose. But I wasn't made to feel, when I did lose, as though I had forfeited anything. My mom was still happy to be there, watching me give all I had; nothing was going to rock her faith in me. No matter how well I did, she refused to set me up with specific expectations, like "With your times, you should definitely win the individual medley today." She refused to have an agenda for me. My dad, of course, had no agenda other than to socialize with the other parents and have a good time, and whether I won or lost, he would manage to enjoy being at a meet all day. Neither my teammates nor my friends based their friendship with me on my performance. My coach never punished me with cruel words or workouts. If Mike had certain expectations of me, he had the sense to keep them to himself so that I never felt I'd let him down. When I lost, we'd analyze together where I went wrong, and how I could learn from the mistake. Then I'd put it behind me, because there was no way to go back. Afterward, I'd take from it what I needed and go forward.

Or as Justin used to tell himself after shooting a bad arrow, "Just load another one, because it's down there. Stay focused. If you lose, it's not the end of the world."

Even if I thought, for an hour or so after a jarring defeat, that my failure *was* the end of the world, my parents wouldn't let me believe it for long. My dad would go into overdrive to remind me that just *life* was worth celebrating, just the fact that we were together and the hard work was over for the day. Swimming alone was worth a pizza party. My mom took the opposite tack: win or lose, I came home to the same routine, the same family rituals, the same chores, the same joys. Her job, as she saw it, was to provide total consistency, and because she did, I never confused how I swam with who I was. No matter what happened in the pool, I'd be the same person out of it, with the same support group feeling the same love for me regardless.

Swimming was never an index of my self-worth; my family was the only index I looked to, and it never changed.

Whenever I felt people's expectations as pressure, I'd think about my family and friends, the things we did together that had nothing whatsoever to do with swimming, and I'd realize those relationships would all stay exactly the same whether I won or lost.

Not surprisingly, winners like Dan Jansen and Bonnie Blair make a point of telling themselves the same thing whenever pressure starts confusing what's at stake. It's what carried Bonnie through every competitive crunch point. "It was the comfort of knowing my family and my coach were there, that their expectations were virtually nil—and that if I failed, they'd still be there, saying, 'Well, try again tomorrow.'"

Whatever happens in the next minute, Dan told himself as he crouched at the starting line for his last race, *I'm going to wake up tomorrow and be the same person.* He always had that perspective, he says, ever since he was a child: skating mattered, but it wasn't everything. "Are we rich?" he'd asked his parents once, and they said, "Yes, because we have you nine children." There was more to life than skating around a rink, as his dad had once been forced to remind him. And after his sister Jane died of leukemia the morning he was to compete in Calgary, Dan never lost his perspective on his sport again.

"I thought I'd had the right perspective before I went out that morning to race," he says. "But deep down I had this drive that could never be satisfied. After Jane's death, though, I knew, no matter what, that all I can do is give my best. And I would be satisfied."

Dan, Bonnie, and I all hated the idea of letting people down—our teammates, our coaches, our parents. Whenever we lost, we all imagined we were. And yet at the same time, we knew deep down that these were precisely the people who were incapable of feeling let down by how we performed. Dan says his first thought, as he crossed the finish line there in Lillehammer and saw his new world record on the board, was *Now we can finally celebrate!* "That was what *I* felt—they didn't!" says Dan. "They'd come to all four Olympics, expecting a celebration, and it kept happening that I didn't quite make it. I felt bad, like I was letting them down. But what a ridiculous thought: That's not why they were there. *I* felt that way; they didn't, ever. They were proud of me when I won, but they were never disappointed in me when I lost."

Dot Richardson remembers warming up with a teammate of hers soon after she'd signed on with the woman's professional softball team as a thirteen-year-old. "I made a bad throw, so I said, 'Oh! Sorry, Mary Lou!' And Mary Lou said to me, 'Don't ever say sorry to me again, because I know you didn't mean to throw it like that. I know you're doing your best.'

"That episode with Mary Lou," Dot explains, "was like my parents saying, 'We love to watch you play!' You realize they love you for you. They know you're giving everything you have."

Of course, says Dot, you don't realize that at first. "You want your parents there, and you want to make them happy," she explains. "You want their approval. But that builds up fear: If you do bad, you think you've let them down. You think what you do is what makes you who you are. You grow out of that only by having people around you reassure you, win or lose, that it doesn't matter."

BY THE TIME I was ten, I think I knew the only person whom I could disappoint with a bad swim was myself, because my expectations of myself were higher than anybody else's. I set the upper limit. I determined my own goals. Maybe this was an inborn trait, as some people have argued; I'd argue that setting personal goals, having personal dreams, is an inborn trait of every child, only some children take longer than others to narrow the focus. It's parents who rush in to fill the seeming vacuum with their own specific ambitions who make it impossible for their children to ever determine and pursue their own.

Since I was in charge of the expectation level, my attitude, before a race, was almost the exact opposite of fear: I turned over the possibility of amazing myself. *Well, just how fast can I go today?* I'd think as I mounted the block. I had my personal best times I wanted to beat; I thought about those. I didn't think about my competitors, about their race. I focused on myself.

No Deposit, No Return

When I did lose, I understood it happened for a reason. Defeat meant I hadn't had enough experience going into the race. It never meant that I was doomed to fail again, that I had fallen into some impossible rut. Quite the contrary: I was in control. Failure just showed me what, exactly, I had to work on—my stroke, my dive, my turns. If I did the work, I had nothing to fear. If I did the work, I'd see the payoff.

Or as Mike loved to say, "You put your money in the bank, you make your deposit, and then at the end of the year, it's yours to spend. No deposit, no return."

He told us that nearly every practice; we should have had T-shirts made up with that printed on it: *No deposit, no return.* Put in the work, and you will have no room to doubt yourself up on those blocks.

He was absolutely right. Before every race, in those nail-biter moments before the gun went off, I knew I had put in the work. I knew I had made all the deposits. There wasn't a day on my calendar that didn't prove it: I could look there and see exactly how many days I swam, and how many goal times I had achieved. I could see how fast I was to the fraction of a second, and I always had before me the times I wanted to achieve, pasted on my bathroom mirror, staring me in the eye. I had given myself goal times to strive for at a very young age, and as I made each one, I continued to set them higher. I never eased up on myself, never missed an opportunity to make a deposit, for the very reason that one single episode of not giving my all would open up a chink in my mental armor for doubt to creep in.

There were times—plenty of them—where I'd hear the alarm go off, open my eyes, see *4:14 A.M.* on the clock, and turn over the possibility of just rolling over and going back to sleep. I lived to sleep. I craved it. I deserved it. Nothing, at that moment, would feel better. Nothing was more tempting. No one would deny me: it was *my* choice to go to practice, it was *my* dream of someday going to the Olympics, and that meant getting up at this god-awful hour. My mom certainly wouldn't have minded staying in bed.

But I said to myself, *If I don't go this morning, there will be plenty of others who will, and then it will be tougher for me to stand on those blocks and say, I'm ready.* No deposit, no return.

And I figured if I was going to go to practice, I was going to make the most of it. I treated each practice like a meet. Whoever was in the lane next to me, I'd make a pact with myself to beat. Never mind if they were doing something completely different than I was—kicking, drilling—I was going to touch the wall first. That way, every day I saw myself winning. The more I saw myself winning, the more I was able to visualize myself winning in a meet.

During my troubled fourteenth year, that's what the sports psychologist my dad hired got me to do: visualize winning. Remind myself how much I loved to race. Feel the sensation of flying on the surface of the water. See myself touching the wall, touching it first. See my times on the board improve.

It wasn't hard to do this; I was forever playing a little videotape in my head, seeing myself coming from behind, seeing myself surprise everybody, hearing the announcer describe the upset. It became my mental habit. It became as reflexive as my butterfly.

Of course, this visualizing would never have worked if all I ever did was imagine how it would look to win. I didn't need to merely imagine: I could draw the image from reality. I could see just how it had looked to touch out all my competitors, because I'd done it. I went to practice so I could give myself the image I wanted to see in my head up on those blocks before a race. I pushed myself hard so that I would know exactly what I was capable of: not the extent of my ability—that was always open-ended—but what I could do at the very least. Mike, as I've said, made a point of having us know even without a clock what our bodies could do. Richard, too, constantly pushed us to set goals for ourselves that we thought were unattainable, and then he'd push us in practice until we made them. "See? See how fast you can go?" he loved to gloat. That strategy accomplished two things: we knew exactly where we stood, but not exactly how far we could go. He made us prove to ourselves that what we thought was our maximum output was actually our minimum.

So we went into competition dead certain that whatever we had done in practice was surely the very least we could do in the heat of competition. Richard never tried to fool us into thinking we'd achieved more than we had. Like Mike before him, Richard understood that we couldn't possibly be mentally bullet-proof if even for a moment we found out we weren't what we thought we were. Knowledge of our ability was the first and most important defense we had against the pressure demons. And the only way to come by that knowledge was through experience. A *lot* of it.

No one can hand an athlete self-confidence. No one can give someone self-esteem. No one can make a person believe she has the right stuff, the stuff to win. An athlete can only be granted the experience to find out for herself. She must prove it to herself by doing it. Inner arrogance—the voice that says, *I can win this*—isn't something an athlete can believe just because she wants to, or because her parents want her to. She has to have shown herself, through experience, what is possible.

When Bonnie Blair had to beat out Christa Rathenburger

right after Christa had set a world record in the 500, what she drew on was the fact that in practice, she had clocked an even faster time than Christa's world record. She'd also beat Christa when they had raced head to head, so she had the visual to draw on, as well—the image, taken from reality, of pulling ahead of this particular skater. That knowledge was her mental edge. She went up to her coach and said, "I think I can beat that time she posted! I won in my test run!"

"I know," her coach said. But Bonnie could see he wasn't so sure.

"He was way more nervous than I was," she recalls, "too nervous for me to be around. So I skated away from him. I had this calming thought within me, that if I could skate the race I knew I was capable of, I could beat her."

Bonnie stayed away from the media, too. "That's how I focused," she says. "I let their expectations go in one ear and out the other. I kept within me what I thought I was capable of doing. I would never have gone up to some reporter and said, 'I can win.' My goals were for me to know only."

Historically, Christa was a faster starter than Bonnie. But at the 100-meter mark, Bonnie heard the announcer give the split time: she'd completed that part of the race .02 seconds faster than Christa. *If I'm close to perfect from here, I can beat her,* Bonnie recalls thinking. When she crossed the finish line, there it was on the clock: Bonnie had won by two one-hundredths of a second.

I'VE WONDERED AT times if I would have had the same mental toughness if there had been another swimmer who was better than me in practice so that I didn't get that satisfaction of winning every day. Would I have been as good when it came time to race for real if I hadn't had the mental visual? Would I have had that inner arrogance, that kick-ass confidence?

I have to say yes. Because it wasn't winning, per se, that gave it to me. It was setting challenges for myself, and then mastering them. Any challenges, anywhere. I challenged myself outside of the pool as much as I did in it.

Swimming was always part of a much bigger picture: I wanted to get into Stanford so I could swim with the best, and I wanted a full scholarship. No one had planted that goal in my head; my mom just consistently encouraged me to shoot high, and to me, Stanford was as high as I could imagine. So I never took remedial math or deadbeat English. I wanted to take auto shop, but since Stanford required calculus, I took that instead. My math teacher, Mr. Holmes, always put the seniors' names up on his board with the college they'd gotten into, and I wanted my name up there: *Summer Sanders, Stanford.* And getting that scholarship was going to be like getting a best time.

I put myself through so many tests, day in and day out, that I proved to myself I could meet any goal that was put before me. I could have no fear of failure to cripple me, no matter how intense the pressure. With each win, in practice or in competition, I grew even surer. Worrying about failure wasn't even a thought on the horizon. Each race was only an opportunity to see what I could do, to see my hard work pay off. Like Mike said, I was there for the experience. And like he promised, at the end of each season, I had a ton of deposits there for the spending.

That became my edge.

I distinctly remember when it dawned on me that I could harness this pride and make it work for me. I was at a Far Western meet, up against Becky Beisman in the breaststroke. Becky had beaten me so many times in this event in previous meets, I should have been scared. I could remember, in past meets, thinking how great she was. I could remember dwelling on how many times she had touched me out. But this time I didn't think about Becky and how tough she was. I didn't run the tape where she touched me out. I might have, out of sheer exhaustion; it was the end of the meet, and I was so tired I could barely get out of bed in the morning. But instead I thought about all the big rivals I'd beaten in previous meets. I focused on how I'd touched them out, and how once I'd beaten them, I never lost to them again. I reminded myself I had the experience of winning in countless tough situations, situations just like this one, where I faced a rival just when I was feeling my most tired. I decided it was time to cash in on that experience. I couldn't bear the thought of being touched out again by just a little bit. I wasn't going to let it happen.

I can do this, I thought, assuming my position on the block next to Becky's.

As my mother used to say, when it's neck and neck, the person who wants it most will touch the wall first. I beat Becky that day, and I never lost to her again.

Knowing I could win, knowing I had the right stuff, was entirely different from *expecting* to win. Mike allowed me to keep my "Let's just see how fast I can swim today" mind-set, my la-di-da attitude. He saw no reason to alter my casual out-look—that swimming and winning was more like a big party with my good friends, a party I didn't want to miss out on by not giving it my all. He was in no rush to get me to take myself seriously. He trusted, as my parents did, that if they allowed me enough range of experience, I would come by that realization all by myself. And I did, all by myself. In the spring of 1988, I went to the Olympic Trials in Texas "just for the experience"— and darn near made the team.

After that, I put pressure on myself to win. The Trials made it clear to me that my goals, high as they were, weren't high enough: I was qualified to shoot for the Olympics, and I wasn't going to waste another moment pretending otherwise. I started showing up for practice as if I were coming to work. Now there was a reason for swimming fast beyond just hanging out with my friends; a lot more people were involved, and I felt the weight of my own potential. I had a job to do, and a lot of work ahead of me. I could expect, at the age of fifteen, to get to the next Olympic Games. It wasn't a subjective assessment. I had the talent. I had the physical training. Most important of all, I had the experience—a ton of it. I felt rich with confidence, because I had a mental bank account full of images of winning. And after losing my Olympic ticket to Seoul by twenty-seven one-hundredths of a second, I had learned just how valuable those visuals were.

No Substitute for Experience

I've seen the video replay of my near-miss performance at the '88 Trials, and it's all right there. You can see exactly when and where my mind got in the way of my race: right as I pushed off for the last lap of the last leg of the 200 individual medley.

I had swum the first three legs—butterfly, back, breast—

exactly as Mike had coached me for this particular race. *Just go as fast as you can from the very beginning, and if you die, you die— but at least you gave it all your effort.* Never mind that four days ago, in the finals of the 400 IM, I had come in fifteen whole seconds after Janet Evans and had to listen to her audience explode as I struggled for the wall; I wasn't thinking about that. Never mind that all my competitors were very tough, very experienced; I wasn't even watching them from my lane. I was focusing on my race. I was focusing on giving everything I'd given in practice, and more. By the time I hit the freestyle leg, I was cruising. I was *flying*. I felt great. I was having a *great* time out there.

But then, after I pushed off for the last lap and took my first breath, I glanced over to lanes four through six. I couldn't see a soul. I was in first place. And that scenario simply wasn't in my mental plan.

I had visualized a great race, but I had not visualized winning. So to be in the lead, this late in the race, totally freaked me out. It broke my focus. I started thinking all the wrong things. For instance, I didn't have enough clothes to get to South Korea. If I qualified in the Trials, I'd go straight to Hawaii and then to Seoul, and I hadn't packed for that kind of outcome. I told myself the stupidest things. *I don't have enough underwear! I don't have a passport! What will I do about school!*

At my next breath, everyone was at my feet. I started windmilling frantically. The faster I moved my arms, the less *oomph* I got out of the water. As I motored toward the wall, two girls passed me. I finished twenty-seven one-hundredths of a second behind them, in third place. Only the first two would go to Seoul.

I wasn't disappointed, though. Far, far from it: I was wildly excited to have placed third. I had walked in there, not self-doubting, exactly, but intimidated, because every girl there seemed bigger, tougher, stronger, more experienced, and maybe even more ready than I was. They looked like they belonged in a qualifying event for the Olympics. I didn't feel like I did.

I can remember the scene in the "ready room," where all sixteen competitors were to report ten minutes before the race began. It was just a room with chairs lined up in lane order, with someone there to check us in, but it made me so nervous I decided I needed to check in and get out. All the girls sitting in there wore shoes, sweats, and robes with hoods; some were wearing Walkmans, so they were completely tuned out, and I remember the top-seeded girl who actually placed first that day—as if she weren't already intimidatingly tough—spat on the wall! I felt out of my league, and I looked it. I looked like some kid walking into a summer rec swim pool. I was barefoot, with a tie-dyed T-shirt and cutoff jeans over my suit and a towel slung over my shoulder. When it came time to race I was so nervous, I almost stopped breathing. But I remembered what Mike had said, about pulling a no-brainer, and that's exactly what I went out and did.

So when I reached the wall and realized I had crushed these tough babes and bettered my time by three seconds, I was *stoked.* I swam halfway down the pool for a warm-down, got out, and hugged my coach. It wasn't until we'd walked over to the other side, where they replayed the race on a movie screen half the size of the pool, that I saw just how huge a lead I had had.

That was painful. But it was the kind of pain where I was

laughing at the same time. It was not devastating. I just couldn't believe it: I saw the other girls catch up to me; I saw myself struggling. I hadn't realized how close I was to winning. Even my parents thought I had come in second, it was so fingernail close.

In the end, I realized, I *was* there for the experience, and I'd gotten it. After those Trials, I wasn't going to be scared, not ever again. I was never again going to think, *I don't deserve to be in this lane next to this proven athlete.*

Failing to make the Seoul Olympic team was the beginning of my success, ironically enough. It vaulted me into a whole new arena, one in which I got national attention and went on international meets. United States Swimming invited me to participate as one of twelve members on the Junior National team going to Estonia—me, a sophomore, invited to go to Finland and Estonia on behalf of my country! I was so fired up. I called my dad at his office from his house, where I'd ripped open the letter at the mailbox, and even though he was right in the middle of a root canal, he got all fired up too. Before the trip, I was issued tons of cool gear—a USA parka, at least four sets of complete sweats, a camera, maybe twenty T-shirts and shorts, and gym bags to carry it all in—and that made me so proud, I can still remember thinking, *Wow, I've made it! I like the feeling, and I want to make it even more!*

My attitude during practice was a scary thing. *I'm gonna kick your ass to get where I want to get, every single day* was how I thought. I could be friends with all my teammates, but once I got in the pool, I wanted more than anything to beat them. And each day that I did, each meet that I met my expectations, each time I put my mental toughness to the test and pulled out a victory—my deposits added up so that I had even more to spend on the next big moment.

The moments got bigger and bigger. The wins did more and more for my attitude. At the age of seventeen, I was practically bulletproof with confidence.

Love Those Nerves

"But the *pressure*," people have said to me a thousand times. "How do you deal with pressure like that? Aren't you a nervous wreck?"

Nerves made me run to the toilet every five minutes. Nerves made my heart bang against my chest. Nerves made me shake from head to toe. But I learned, from feeling them over and over before countless competitions, that nerves are not a sign of anything until you give them meaning. I never interpreted my trembling or constant need to pee as a sign of unreadiness; that wouldn't have made sense, because I *was* ready. I'd gone to every practice, pushed myself to the max at every opportunity, put myself to challenges outside the pool as well as in it. If nerves made my adrenaline flow, that was good: you can't perform at your peak without adrenaline. So as soon as I felt my heart race, and my breathing change, and my bladder fill up, I felt *ready.*

I learned, as Justin Huish says, to *love* that nervous feeling. Justin remembers all too vividly back when he didn't.

"I had good form from day one," he says of his first years in the sport. "I could shoot tens. But from practice to competition, I'd get too nervous to shoot my good shot. I tried different mental techniques. I pictured shooting tens. I worked with my coach on convincing myself I could do it.

"What's hard about archery," he explains, "is that if you shake just a little, you miss the bull's-eye. I'd get all fired up, but I wouldn't know how to eat up that energy and use it for good. It made me feel ill. My coach said, 'You gotta learn to love it. You think you're nervous now? How do you think you're going to feel that last round, when you're down to your last arrow and it's never been more important how you shoot?' "

It finally came to that. Justin made the final cut during the Arizona Cup in 1993. His first round of head-to-head shooting, he drew Sebastian Flute, the 1992 reigning gold medalist from France. Justin wasn't really nervous until it got down to a sudden-death, one-arrow finish. They both shot an eight. By the second arrow, Justin recalls, the nerves kicked in big-time. "I could not pull my bow back," he says. "My knees were knocking. I felt woozy. I shot a four; he shot a nine."

For the next two years, Justin shot decent but not world class. "It was a confidence thing," he says. "I kept saying, 'These guys are better than me!' "

And then he broke through.

"It just happened, over time," he says. "Maybe it was experience. One day I told myself, 'I love this nervousness!' and I *did.* I told myself it was like that first date, that high-life feeling you come to love. The one time I went to a local tournament and didn't get nervous, I shot really bad! Nervousness gives me that feeling that I'm pumped, that I care."

Not feeling nervous—that's when a competitor knows something is wrong. Debi Thomas didn't feel nervous going out into the Olympic rink for her final performance against Katarina Witt—"I had practiced so well, I was so prepared, I didn't have to do my typical now-you've-got-to-pull-it-all-together routine," she explains—and the result was catastrophic. So when she had turned professional, and was competing in the World Professional Championships, she reminded herself, no matter how well she'd skated in practice, she couldn't afford not to do her normal pump-up. "In practice I'd skate seventy-five percent of what I'm capable of skating," she explains, "and then I'd psych myself, saying, 'I gotta get my act together.' Then I'd do the pacing, the visualizing, the telling myself I could do it—and in competition, I'd skate amazingly well.

"I learned from the Olympics, obviously," she says. "Nerves are a good thing."

Going up against Janet Evans in the 1990 Goodwill Games, I was scared to death. The day of our race, every five minutes I had to rush off and pee. The event was the 400 IM—her race, the one she'd taken the gold in two years before. We both couldn't wait for it to be over; in the ready room we talked about how we couldn't wait for it to be over, because it was so tough, and because we both knew we were going to make it even tougher for each other. Then we left the ready room, paraded around the pool, and took our positions.

And then—oooh yes. That familiar feeling. *A reserve of pee just to piss me off.*

I had to pee so badly I couldn't hold it. We were at the blocks, where we started splashing ourselves down, so I thought I'd let out just a little. But I didn't have that kind of control; I couldn't stop. So I swung my legs around to the grates and started splashing myself like a maniac, praying the whole time that I'd be finished before they were done announcing each lane and called us up on the blocks.

Now, imagine, letting go right there on the edge of the pool in front of thousands.

I cannot believe I'm peeing, I thought.

I hope these people don't know what I'm doing.

And then: *I can't wait to tell Heather about this! I cannot wait to tell everyone about this!*

Suddenly, the whole thing struck me as so funny, I calmed down. I'd been so stressed about competing against Janet Evans that relaxing my control like that was a grounding moment.

I got off to a terrific start. In the backstroke leg of the race, Janet started to catch me. But I was concentrating on making the second lap of each leg faster than the first. That left me thinking, by the time I pushed off for the freestyle, *Do I have enough left to hold off a double gold medalist in the distance free?* As I turned for my very last lap, I saw she was a good body length and a half behind me. That's when it hit me, that I could win this thing.

I'm going to do this, I thought, *I want to win, and by God, I can.*

She came on really strong that last lap, but there was no catching me. I wanted this win, I had earned this win, I'd suffered the embarrassment of unbelievable nerves for this win, and no one, not even Janet Evans, was going to deny me this win.

After that, nerves took on a whole new meaning: They signaled I was *psyched.* They became my badge of mental courage.

At that first bladder attack, I filled up with inner arrogance. Nerves didn't make me edgy; nerves were my edge.

The Secret of Inner Calm

During my freshman and sophomore years at Stanford, in fact, for the annual NCAAs I put in the best performances of my life, precisely because I was mentally about the toughest I've ever been in my life. It wasn't just that I had harnessed my nerves; swimming with those twenty-four girls at Stanford, the cream of the crop, many of them my best friends, I felt part of something larger, something virtually unstoppable. As a team, it became easy to focus on what we were going to do to the competition—never on what they were going to do to us. Our attitude was *KICK ASS*. Not that we'd ever say such a thing out loud, but you could feel it. We positively radiated it. That was the final installment to my mental toughness—belonging to a group brimming over with confidence, each of us having earned it individually before pooling it together as a team.

It made us fierce competitors—so fierce, each of us would take even the slightest opportunity to vent some of our competitive fire, to strut our stuff, even if it was our closest friend we were racing against.

One time, right before the '92 NCAA 200 IM, a bunch of reporters interviewed me about how I was going to do. I gave the standard answer—"It's so great just being here, and I hope to have fun out there, and just swim my best," or something equally lame. Then I heard one of my best friends, Nicole, and her coach murmur something under their breath, and they both started laughing. I instantly assumed they were talking about the 200 IM. So what I *thought* I heard them say was, "We'll see about that."

For all I know, Nicole and her coach were talking about going to McDonald's. But I chose to hear it differently. I chose to turn it into a challenge, something I could draw on to fuel my fire—and Nicole picked up on it. We got in the water, she and I, knowing exactly how huge each other's attitude was, and by the time we got out, we'd both bettered our times and literally smashed the American record (which had been mine), and which I had now reclaimed.

We were both such proven talents at that point, we were looking for something beyond winning. We were past seeing competition as a test we might fail; instead, we saw it as our opportunity to shine, an opportunity we'd worked for our whole life. All we'd been born with, all our parents and coaches had taught us, all the experience we'd collected, all the training we'd endured—all that came together in the heat of intense competition. And when it did, it was such a thing of beauty, we wanted more than anything to share it.

Inner arrogance is not, then, what helps a true champion "cope" with pressure; inner arrogance is what drives her to seek it out, because pressure is what brings out her very best. An athlete needs to understand that wanting to give her very best is not arrogant, not selfish: in fact, it's the most selfless attitude. Acknowledging a gift is to acknowledge that there is a debt. What's selfish is *not* looking for the opportunity to share the gift, or *not* taking the opportunity when it's granted, out of fear.

Dot Richardson explained this to me when I asked her how it must have felt, stepping up to the plate during the last inning of the first-ever Olympic women's fast-pitch softball game, down by a run, and one out away from losing. "Wasn't the pressure just awful?" I asked her.

"I never felt the pressure," she said. "I was where I'd always wanted to be. I had total confidence in my teammates; this was *my* opportunity. We were the chosen few, the fifteen who would represent all those who had ever dreamed of this moment. I felt excitement, not pressure, because I was being given the opportunity to express my talent."

She expressed it, all right. She hit a home run. The United States won. Dot took home a gold medal.

And if she had blown it?

"I'd rather have tried," she said, "and gotten out, than never to have been given the chance to try at all."

She told me about one of the times she was denied the opportunity. It was when her team had made Nationals, and they were in Omaha, playing through a bout of food poisoning to try and take the championship. In the bottom of the seventh, with her team losing by one run, Dot came up to bat with two outs and was intentionally walked. The next girl hit the pitch but was thrown out at first. That ended the game; the team lost the championship. "I didn't feel relieved at all that it was her and not me," says Dot. "When I saw her make the last out, that's when I learned I'd rather have been given the chance, and gotten out, and felt that pain, than never have gotten the chance to try."

That same attitude carries over into her career as an orthopedic surgeon. "I don't feel the 'I can'ts' in surgery," says Dot. "I'm almost to the point where I want to say, 'I want you to believe in me, because I care for you, and I know I'm going to give you my best.'"

A true champion doesn't fear the crunch point, says Dot. She doesn't hope or try to avoid it: she looks for it, because she knows it's a rare thing, a privilege, to be granted the opportunity to share her gift.

Inner Arrogance and Inner Calm

While I was pacing from tension, watching Dan Jansen wait for the gun to skate his final race in his final Olympics, Dan himself was at peace.

"I knew what I had accomplished over the years," he says. "I'd been a world champion, a World Cup champion, a world-record holder, the first person to break the thirty-six-second barrier in the 500 meter. I knew I'd be measured by other people by what happened here in the next minute or so, but I tried not to look at it as a deciding factor, the next 1:12:43. I knew people would say, 'Oh, he's the best ever, but he couldn't do it under pressure in the Olympics'—well, success is a very personal thing. As I prepared for that final race, I truly felt that peace of knowing I was the best."

This is what inner arrogance and mental toughness and hungering for competition ultimately earn you: inner calm.

I can't stress enough, however, that coming by this mind-set is a process, and a long one. You can't make someone believe in themselves without giving them the chance to explore their own abilities, any more than you can give a girl self-esteem by rigging a race so that she wins. So many of the parenting books talk about self-esteem and self-confidence, especially in young girls, as something inborn and fragile, something you can ruin by saying the wrong thing or by not sparing them negative experiences. In my book, that's totally backward. Self-confidence isn't inborn, it's earned. You can't handpick the experiences for your child that you think will nurture her self-image: the experiences that teach her the most about herself and her abilities are usually the unanticipated ones, the tough ones, even the ordeals. You *can* ruin self-esteem, but not by *failing* to spare your child the hard knocks; it's *stepping in* that robs a child of her confidence, that sends the message "You're too fragile or incompetent to handle it yourself."

That's the message parents send who are overeager to see their child make it.

Parents need simply to value experience—the good, the bad, and even the ugly—and not fear it themselves. They need to trust in its teaching power. They need to live their own lives by way of example, not fearfully, not worrying about screwing up, but head-on, with the confidence they can make the best of even bad situations. It's not the parents' job to edit or censor what events come a child's way; rather, it's the parents' job to teach, by example, how to handle whatever pitch life throws, especially the curveballs. A kid who sees that demonstrated is more likely to step up to the plate herself. A strikeout won't set her back; instead, she knows it will prepare her to better handle the next chance at bat.

I was lucky enough to have parents transform misfortune right before my very eyes. One day my mother was a wife and mother living in her dream home; the next, she was divorced, jobless, and living in a rental whose roof leaked. But she turned that failure into a stepping-stone toward personal achievement, toward an independence and confidence she'd never known before. One day my dad had it all: his beautiful family, a home he'd built with his own hands, and a thriving dental practice; the next, he had all the trappings of that life but none of its comforts, except for our company during the six months we lived with him. And yet he rebounded from this failure by becoming our father, rather than the guy who only supported us financially.

Even my grandpa Charlie, my dad's dad, who practically lived with us half the year, was a living lesson in making bad apples into applesauce. I can still remember his stories of growing up in the Depression; of surviving a tornado that wiped out his town, in Xenia, Ohio; of driving west until he got to Hollywood, where he found contracting work for the studios; of working on the *Spruce Goose* and sharing his lunch with Howard Hughes. He had an amazing life, but only because he took whatever came his way and learned from it.

Firsthand experience is the only way any person learns how to handle adversity. Yet I see so many parents denying their children that firsthand experience, by editing out what they deem "won't be good for their self-esteem"—I guess out of their own fear of failure. My grandpa, my parents, and my coaches all trusted that personal experience would give me everything I would need to get wherever I was going. They didn't decide for me what was worthwhile and what was a mistake. They allowed me to make decisions like quitting swimming or drinking at a party or shelving my sport for a career in broadcasting. They didn't step in to keep me from screwing up, and they didn't punish me when I did. Some decisions I made were downright awful, but since no grown-up stepped in to bail me out, I learned how to handle the worst. I learned I *could* handle the worst. I learned I was in control. If I did the work, if I saw in every setback a lesson I couldn't have come by any other way, then I knew I would eventually win. Winning increased my confidence, my sense of control, until I was so brimming with inner arrogance, I hungered for intense competition. I'd get nervous not out of fear, then, but out of excitement, anticipating the moment in which I'd get to bring together in one glorious display all my talent, training, and true grit.

Deep down, I had that precious inner calm.

Going into my fifth and final race of the '92 Games, I was practically Mister Rogers, I was so mellow. *Don't make this complicated,* I kept telling myself. I reminded myself of two things: The 200 butterfly was my best event—I had proven I could swim it faster, longer, than anybody in the world. And this was the last race, the last time I had to draw on everything I had. I could see the light at the end of the tunnel.

It was the kind of calm I broke through to from sheer exhaustion. I'd swum a total of eight races—no one else in the pool had qualified for as many events as I had, so no one else had swum as many races. There wasn't an emotion in the human spectrum I hadn't fully experienced by that point—excitement, nerves, worry, stress, doubt, disappointment, joy, and wonderment that I was even competing in the Olympics. For each of those races I had mentally prepared differently: I remember trying to get relaxed for the first one, the 400 IM, by going into this place in the Village where you could rent CDs and lie down in an air-conditioned room. I listened to Van Morrison, telling myself to save my nerves for when they'd really serve me best—for the 200 IM. That race was so tough, I knew I had to be ready to *kill.* I psyched myself up for it by doing the classic rock concert head-banging routine, telling myself, *You're TOUGH, you CAN do this, you've gone through thousands of races, you're the TOUGHEST!* And it worked: I swam my best 200 IM ever and set an American record, even though it wasn't enough to take the gold.

So going into my final event, I just couldn't bring myself to the same emotional boil. I was spent. That's why Richard came up to ask me, right before I dove in to warm up, "Are you *focused?*"

After I'd done my warm-up set, I climbed out of the pool and found a bathroom to change into my racing suit. It was some random women's room, and there wasn't another soul around. I stood there in my racing suit, staring at my face in the mirror. I said to myself, out loud, with this kind of half-smile on my face, *Go out there and swim for YOURSELF.*

Be tough—but have fun with this!

It's the toughest thing, but you can do this.

Do it for yourself.

It's the last race. Just go out and swim.

Do it for yourself.

I talked to my reflection like this over and over until the half-smile turned into a full smile. Then I thought, *What the hell are you doing?* because I'd never done that before.

I snapped out of it and headed out to join the other swimmers, waiting to go out into the arena.

I had a few minutes while the announcer introduced all the lanes, so I thought about the people I loved who would love me back no matter what: my parents, my brother, my friend Heidi, and my coaches, Richard and Mike. I looked up at this huge banner that said "BARCELONA OLYMPICS 1992" and I thought, *This is the last time I'll be swimming in these Olympics in Barcelona, so give it everything you've got.*

I was mentally ready.

And that, as it turned out, was almost entirely what would pull me through my exhaustion to take the gold.

6

Handling Success

There are two kinds of success.

One, we all know about because the media is obsessed with it. It's the Young Talent Out of Nowhere kind of success— Tiger Woods, Martina Hingis, Tara Lipinski, and even me (I was seventeen when I first beat Janet Evans, at that time the fastest American woman).

The other kind is nowhere near as visible. Nobody talks about it; nobody writes about it. The press certainly doesn't take any interest in it. But it's the kind parents *should* take an interest in. It's the kind my own parents valued, and prepared me for really well. It's the true measure of their success as parents, that I got to enjoy it.

Only, I had to survive the sudden, flashy kind of success first. That in itself was a test of all they had done to raise me right.

*   *   *

AFTER WINNING THOSE four medals at the '92 Olympics, I discovered that being a household name and earning big bucks at the age of nineteen was really difficult. You'd think, by the way we all talk about success, that Olympic gold would be some sort of capstone, a liberation from hard work and endless pressure and fear of failure. But it's just the opposite. *Failure* in a way is liberating: you're free to do whatever you want next, because no one's looking, no one's judging you, no one has any expectations. Once you succeed, however, there's only one option open: you must keep winning.

The expectations people piled on me post-Olympics were by far the most constricting of the burdens fame made me shoulder. They made me feel like I was swimming with a forty-pound diver's belt around my waist. I couldn't even get in the water without being reminded that everybody was looking at me to see if I could uphold my title. Public scrutiny had never bothered me before, but in June of 1993, a year after Barcelona, as I stood on the blocks at a meet in Fort Lauderdale poised to swim the 200 butterfly, all I could think of was what my coach had just said to me: "You could be a little leaner." Richard was stating the obvious. I was out of shape, or rather, in my case, I *had* a shape—real cheeks, and not just in my face. Having that pointed out to me would have been okay if I'd just been another swimmer in another swim meet. But right at that moment I heard the announcer introduce me to the whole arena as "OLYMPIC AND WORLD CHAMPION, SUMMER SANDERS!" and I could feel all eyes on me, fat me, an out-of-shape former Olympian who was about to swim her gold-medal event.

It was unbearable. In the water, I felt like a pig. I came in fourth. I didn't even change out of my suit after the race. I walked back to my hotel and said to myself, "That's it. I'm taking the summer off." Competing wasn't fun anymore. That didn't bode well. Practice can definitely be a drag, but competing should *always* be fun. I was no longer swimming "for the experience," as Mike used to insist. I *had* the experience, but it wasn't working in my favor anymore. The more I knew going into a race, the more I thought, and the more I thought, the more I thought the wrong thing up there on the blocks. I didn't know how to get back to that place where I could just go and swim and wonder if that good-looking boy Scott was watching me kick ass. I yearned for those la-di-da days when I'd breeze in for practice or a meet after taking in a movie or goofing off with my friends, when I could literally throw on my suit, go out, and pull a no-brainer. Those days were gone. Huge, public success had made me hyperaware of myself, of all that was riding on me. I had trouble concentrating on my own race, on the moment at hand. All I could think was *I am the winner of four Olympic medals, and I have to win.*

I had no other identity outside of swimming.

After Barcelona, I knew what I needed was a real breather, a chance to rest up and get some perspective on my life. I kept promising myself I was going to do it. But I didn't quit; I couldn't even cut back without setting up deadlines for my return. *I'll take the summer off, but dig in in September,* I told myself after Fort Lauderdale. Heading into my spring semester, I said, *I'll skip morning practices, but I'll still do afternoons.* There was no reality of an existence outside of swimming. I could fiddle with my practice schedule, but who was I kidding? There was no leaving my sport, not for the foreseeable future, anyhow. I was trapped.

Success had robbed me of what my parents had struggled so many years to protect: a life and an identity outside of my sport and a life of career options. The Olympics made me a swimmer, period. So I came to feel that's all I was.

Part of me recognized that the only way out of this box was to start over, to embrace a new challenge, in a new arena, where expectations couldn't follow me, or at least where I felt I had a little more latitude for failure. But having worked so hard to "arrive," I didn't see how I could leave. I couldn't quit and risk people saying, "Oh, she'll never do anything again."

So I elected to stay in the arena where I'd proven myself successful, even though it felt like a prison.

And that was only one of the prisons I found success had put me in.

After Barcelona, I found that I couldn't just be myself. I could only be That Person Who Won. I'd be introduced to someone as That Person, and then I'd have to talk about my swimming, which I absolutely hated, because I could see the look on his or her face change; you could see the barrier go up between us, the distancing effect my fame had. It made meeting new people very difficult. I'd been shy to start with; I'd never been like my dad, who is so naturally gregarious he can go to a tailgate party without bringing any food. I'd never been like my mom, either, who can't dash into a Las Vegas supermarket for milk without running into ten friends from Nebraska. Still, I'd always operated on the assumption that I could make anyone like me just by being myself. After Barcelona, I could see that was a naive assumption.

That first semester back, I went to a UCLA party. I wanted to go out and have fun, have a few beers, dance—and I couldn't. Somebody yelled my name, and I wheeled around to look—and no one was there. They just wanted to see if it was me, and then they knew it was. I could feel the staring, the pointing. I was vulnerable, suddenly. I thought, *I can't go out there and risk looking spastic; they know who I am, and they're watching me.*

Never before had image been a concern of mine. I'd gone home after the Goodwill Games and, right before the City of Roseville was to honor me with a banquet, I had my wisdom teeth out—it was either have the surgery then and go to the banquet swollen, or be swollen and uncomfortable for a Club Med vacation with my dad and brother (a no-brainer: I chose the banquet rather than ruin my vacation). I was hideous. I looked as though I had a golf ball inside my cheek and under my jaw. I had a hard time closing my lips. And since everything was numb, I couldn't feel the drool. People kept bringing me ice, because they felt so bad for me. But the ice kept dripping on my chest, so the whole right side of my chest was soaking wet. Surely someone who was concerned about her public image wouldn't have risked going on TV in front of the mayor and council members with a big drool spot on her dress. As any Olympic athlete finds, sooner or later, I found public scrutiny very wearing. It can be downright awful if you're not used to it. Justin Huish, who stepped into the Olympics as a virtual newcomer, unknown to anybody but other archers, walked away with two gold medals and, overnight, found his life transformed. "I came home," he told me, "and there were people out in front of my house! Everywhere I went, people recognized me, pointed me out! Friends and family treated me the same, but the fan mail, the phone calls, the huge onslaught of attention—it was scary. I just wanted it all to go back to normal!"

I was a little more prepared than Justin, having had a national camera on me ever since ESPN spotlighted me in the eighth grade for a special on up-and-coming swimmers. But after the Olympics, I discovered I was "on" all the time. Showing up at auditions, speaking in front of hundreds, socializing with banquet guests at corporate functions—just being me was now a job, and an exhausting one. It got so I didn't want to see anybody when I had time off the lecture circuit. It got so I didn't want to meet new people, or venture out to parties where I'd be forced to. I didn't want to have to talk about swimming, or the Olympics, by way of introduction. When someone I was meeting for the first time asked me what I did, I always wished I could say something normal, like "I'm majoring in communications," or later, after Stanford, "I'm teaching second grade."

Almost from the moment I left the Olympic arena, fame isolated me even from my friends and coaches. When I had a victory interview in Bob Costa's studio, I could bring only a few people with me. My parents, of course. And my brother. But who else? I couldn't invite my coaches and many friends who were as much a part of my victory as my family and should have been invited to share in the moment. It hurt me. I wanted a party, and I couldn't have that. It was the first of many instances where I'd be forced to weigh who belonged in the absolute inner circle and who didn't.

In every aspect of my life, I felt success *narrowing* my options rather than opening the door to more. I couldn't be who I felt I was; I couldn't do what I used to feel free to do; I couldn't hang out with people who weren't my absolute dearest friends.

Worst of all, my financial success confused the easy, straight-forward relationships I had with the people closest to me: my brother, my parents, my coaches. At nineteen, I was making more money than most parents. Part of me wanted to ask my parents, "Can you put this in some place for later? When I'm *supposed* to be making this kind of money?" Another part of me thought having money was pretty cool: I could take my friends to the movies and buy them dinner; I could say to my mom or dad, when the check arrived at the table, "I've got this one."

But very quickly having that much money started limiting me, not freeing me up. I worried that if I spent too freely on my friends and family, they'd expect it and take it for granted. Even worse—much worse—I worried I suddenly *owed* people reimbursement for what they'd given freely. This issue caused me a great deal of torment.

WHAT SAVED ME from this particular hell, this prison I lived in for a year or two after the Olympics, was recognizing that I could still make my own decisions. I had been encouraged to from an early age, and I'd been supported by my parents in every one I'd ever made, bad or good. I was still in the driver's seat. And I knew I could still count on my parents' support.

Handling success is nothing more, I discovered, than choosing to be an active participant. As long as I perceived myself as a victim, someone things just kept happening to, rather than someone who made things happen, success was hell. It was easy to get caught up in the whirlwind, because the press kept fanning it, and so did the money. It was easy to believe I was no longer in charge, that the millions of people who knew my name and watched me swim actually ran my life. It was easy to act like I had no responsibility in the matter, that it was all just happening to me.

Trevor was with me one night at the San Francisco airport when I burst into tears of exhaustion and self-pity. It was all so endless, this business of rushing to make a flight, rushing to make a flight home, rushing right back onto a different airplane to make another flight. I was so sick of it. I hated it.

Trevor heard me out and then shocked me with his response. "You have no idea what *I'm* giving up!" he hissed. "I've been away from my girlfriend for three whole months! Don't expect me to console you, Summer. Maybe next time you'll decide you don't want to do this, and choose differently!"

He was absolutely right: all of it was my choice. If I felt victimized by my own schedule or robbed of my college life because of the endorsement jobs I'd accepted, then I had only myself to blame. Because it all stemmed from a decision I'd made, in the spring of 1992, to give up my eligibility for the swimming scholarship that was to take me through Stanford.

I had made that decision all by myself. No one had told me what to do, because no one had ever been in my situation before. No swimmer had ever given up her athletic scholarship as a sophomore at Stanford and then continued on there (Janet Evans, of course, had gone professional, but she had never had to come back and hang out with Richard as a non–team swimmer).

Richard wasn't about to tell me what to do; instead he put his hands on my shoulders and said, "I knew this would happen. I expected it. I wouldn't accept any less from you. We're going to miss you, but I understand." My parents couldn't possibly tell me what to do, although when I discussed my decision with them, my father leaped on the idea, on the basis that earning a good living, and not passing on good opportunities, was always the right thing to do.

I went with my gut. I was so infatuated with risk, with travel, with new challenges, that I saw speaking engagements and sponsor gigs as wonderful opportunities. I never saw them as the end of my college experience, as the rude shove out of my protected pool life that they would turn out to be. I was never one to overanalyze, or second-guess myself. I was the kind of kid who never erased her first answer on anything.

The endorsement jobs began the minute the Games were over. All summer, and when I resumed classes at Stanford, I went around the world doing work for my sponsors, in addition to keeping up with my studies and swimming my butt off in practice.

I was going places, that's for sure. But I wasn't having any fun. I was no longer on Richard's team. My schoolwork was suffering. My social life was practically nonexistent: I couldn't sustain relationships with many of my campus friends and swimming buddies. I didn't even know the twelve girls I shared a house with. In opting for the lecture circuit—rooms full of strangers assembled to hear me talk—I found I'd denied myself the thing my parents had shown me mattered most: a life of "you-had-to-be-there" moments with my family and friends.

That became painfully clear my first endorsement job—a lavish dinner right after my gold-medal swim in Barcelona. While I milled around making conversation with my sponsors in a huge banquet hall, my friends danced at Studio 54. I thought I could have it all—please the sponsors, be with my family, and later, join my friends. Trevor and I promised to meet up with them after dinner. But when we got there, well after midnight, the line of people waiting to get in wound around the building. When we peered in over the bouncer's shoulder, both of us could see the place was absolutely mobbed. Trevor and I looked at each other. I knew we were thinking the same thing.

"We're never going to find them," I said with a sigh. We didn't try to; we didn't stay. It was one of too many instances where, thinking I could have it all, I wound up with nothing. I was too caught up in the whirlwind to realize that I had to make choices, hard choices—that no amount of success would ever get me off that hook.

Choosing the endorsement business, I inadvertently chose to undermine my swimming career—another instance where I could not have my cake and eat it too. Having turned professional, I was barred from the team Richard coached. Every time I went to practice, I felt my apartness. I would try to pretend nothing had changed, but I knew, when I came in for an afternoon practice, that I'd be faster than the other girls simply because I'd opted not to do morning practices and they'd been pushed to the bone. Or I'd come in and Richard would be talking to the team about a dual meet coming up, one I wasn't allowed to participate in. "Why don't you just get in the pool and start working out?" he'd say, like it was no big deal, " 'cause I've gotta talk to them about tomorrow's meet." So I'd swim alone.

I couldn't travel with the team for NCAA meets, but during home dual meets—swimming and diving competitions put together—I could do what was called an "exhibition swim," where I competed against no one but myself and the clock. Richard would yell, cheer me on, try and make me feel fired up. I felt so uncomfortable out there. Swimming while the audience tried to focus on the divers, I was at best a diversion and at worst a distraction. My only motive to swim my guts out was to get out of the pool to escape the embarrassment faster.

My eligibility decision made me feel more isolated than anything I'd known. I felt like an outcast even the last two months of my sophomore year, although, technically speaking, my non-scholarship status didn't go into effect until the fall of my junior year. Everybody knew I'd elected to go professional. One afternoon in April, when my shoulder was really hurting me, Richard walked me across the street to the training room, the sports medicine center, to a woman I'd seen before announcing my decision. I walked in and the head guy pulled Richard aside. "She's not on scholarship," I could hear him say, "so we can't treat her in here." I was ready to walk right out again, but Richard wasn't about to let that happen. "You know what?" he said, and I could see in his face he was angry: "She's on scholarship till the end of this year, and she's a swimmer. You'll be helping her with her shoulder." Richard was there for me, and I'll always appreciate that, especially during those months before the Olympics. But he also had a team to coach through the next NCAA championships, and there was only so much he could do to make me feel part of something I'd officially given up.

IF THE CONSEQUENCES of my eligibility decision were ones I didn't particularly like—and I regretted them terribly at the time—I nonetheless never felt I had the option to go back on my decision. I'd committed myself, and as a child of divorce, I'd grown up to view a broken commitment as the worst possible thing. My parents had broken their commitment to each other—an unforgivable thing. But I'll give them this: they accepted the consequences, the personal sacrifices, that came from that decision. Trevor and I always understood that having the freedom to choose meant paying the price of living through the consequences of your choice.

My mom, in particular, made that crystal clear. She was a stickler about personal accountability. She wasn't about to let herself off the hook, let alone anybody else. She was ready to blame herself for any number of bad things—what Trevor and I suffered every time we had to switch parents and houses, for example. She never bought into any of that psychobabble that seemed designed to let people get away with murder. She had no time or patience for parents or guidance counselors who insisted on explaining away the awful things children did, as though children could never be held to blame for their own actions. If a kid set fire to paper towels in the school lavatory and nearly burned the school down—this actually happened— my mother felt he should have to pay the piper. "None of this 'We need to get to the root of what's *making* him act out like that,' " my mother told us. "No excuses! He should be punished, period."

The few times I tried to pin blame for something that went wrong on somebody or something else, my mom nipped it right in the bud. Like that swim meet where I didn't see my competitor coming up fast behind me, and took it easy, and lost to her—and then insisted there was something wrong with the timers. No way would my mom let that one fly. Or the time I failed to show up for a reporter who was going to interview me for the *Sacramento Bee*. I was only twelve, but I'd told him I'd be there at the pool, and I went off and did something with my friends instead. My mother really let me have it over that one. Not for a minute would she have allowed me to believe that being twelve years old, or being "just a kid," was any excuse for blowing off an appointment I'd agreed to.

She made sure I knew when I messed up so that I never had any doubt about cause and effect. "This is YOU, Summer," she'd say. "YOU make your life what YOU make of it. You're the only one, to blame or to congratulate. Set your goals, work for them—and you'll get back exactly what you put in."

That was the most important lesson I could have taken from childhood. Because going into that complicated period following my success at the Barcelona Games, I ultimately had to accept my responsibility in the matter. Accepting that I'd caused it meant understanding that I could fix it. The problems success visited upon me—the limitations of money, fame, and massive public expectation—I accepted as my doing, because in doing that, I was acknowledging I had control.

That's the flip side of personal accountability, the incredibly empowering side: to accept blame is to understand you had the power to choose, and that you still do. Initially, the limitations imposed by my success were hard to accept, because I hadn't expected them (whoever expects success to be *difficult?*). But I'd been raised to believe that not anticipating an outcome is no excuse for blaming it on someone or something else. I'd been made to understand, starting with my parents' divorce, that you just make the best of a situation, and don't for a second think you're going to get out of it.

Because here's what happens the minute you accept that it's up to you to make it work, all up to you: whatever you decide, it *does* work out for the best.

Just not immediately.

Getting Wings

Midway through my senior year at Stanford, I took my first step toward freedom—freedom from the mire that Olympic success had made my life. I decided to give up my sport entirely.

It raised a lot of eyebrows among people who didn't know me. *Retire from swimming? Isn't that a little premature?* To that I said, "I've been in that career seventeen years. How long have you been at yours?" I wasn't retiring so much as I was changing careers. Surely, I was entitled.

And again, as with the eligibility decision, it was one I made myself. Yet this time I consulted no one. I didn't need to. The only motivations I had to keep swimming were: (1) habit, (2) money, and (3) a nostalgic desire to be on an Olympic team again—to go to Atlanta for the '96 Games. Those reasons weren't good enough. I'd done everything and more than I ever dreamed of doing, except for breaking a world record. I *could* live without swimming.

I'll never forget the moment when this dawned on me: the relief, the fear, the joy. I remember hopping on my bike, riding as fast as I could back to my dorm, running like a nut up to the fourth floor, and hugging my roommate Heidi. I was so glad to find her there so I could sit her down and tell her my momentous decision. I was crying and laughing at the prospects of my new life.

And I did have a new life, although, again, to my surprise, quitting practice didn't open up the huge chunks of time I'd imagined. I started going to more social events, events I wouldn't have been able to attend if I'd been swimming. I rode my bike, I worked out, I went to classes regularly, I met guys, I started dating one of them seriously, and I made lots of memories with friends outside of the pool. Never once during those final days at Stanford did I feel like going back to swimming, or like I'd made the wrong decision. My family supported me. My friends supported me. I was seizing hold of my life, giving it a direction instead of allowing myself to be just buoyed along by what I'd already done. I was back in the driver's seat. I was ready to leave the arena in which I'd been hugely successful for one where I might fail badly—broadcasting. I had done some commentating for NBC and I'd be doing some more at the World Championships in Rome.

I was ready to take risks again—a very liberating feeling, one I hadn't known in the three years since the Olympics.

What is it that allows any of us to feel comfortable leaving the known for the unknown, the success for the possible failure, the peak for the long hard climb? Matt Biondi says, and I agree, that you've got to feel totally secure, totally safe in one comfort zone, to voluntarily step out of it. That comfort zone can be the success of your own making—my swimming career, for instance. Initially, though, it's the comfort zone not of your own making: it's the comfort zone your parents create for you.

Matt talks about the stability he knew as a kid: his mom was home every day after school, slicing fruit for his snack, making sure the television stayed off; his dad worked for the same employer for thirty-one years; and his town—Moraga, California—was so safe and orderly, it was like *Leave It to Beaver*, "only in color," he says. All that allowed him to take risks elsewhere, and by so doing, to improve himself until he'd created a new comfort zone: success in his chosen sport.

On the surface, the home I grew up in was nothing like Matt's; my parents were anything but *Ozzie and Harriet*. But that's precisely why I have to give my parents an awful lot of credit, because despite their divorce, despite our living arrangements, they managed to provide that all-critical security and stability. Sure there was tremendous upheaval: Every six months Trevor and I moved from one parent's house to the other's. Two days of every year my brother and I grieved like we'd lost a parent, because we had. There was no solution to that grief. We couldn't split the house down the middle, even though I suggested we try.

But in spite of that, or because of it, my parents threw themselves into making up for it, even at tremendous cost to their personal lives. My father never remarried. My mother did, but her first criterion for whom she picked was a guy who wouldn't mind taking second place to her kids, which may explain why that marriage didn't last. My mother saw as her chief responsibility the role of "grounder"—the one who kept things at home absolutely the same, no matter what happened outside of it. It was not a very glamorous job, keeping the routine, honoring the schedule, being a slave to both. But she felt strongly that home should remain a constant, a sanctuary we could count on when there wasn't a stable spot outside of it.

And to a huge degree she succeeded. It was my comfort zone, for sure.

When I first beat Janet Evans during the 1990 Goodwill

Games, the world as I knew it busted wide open. I was suddenly national news. Each time I climbed out of the pool—after the 400 IM, the 200 IM, and the 200 butterfly—the press was all over me. Even when it was all over, they wouldn't leave me alone: I got off the plane in Sacramento, and they swarmed the gate, eager to ask me the same hundred questions I'd already answered. Sure, it was a rush to be suddenly famous and suddenly all over the evening news. But what I most wanted was what only my mom could provide: the peace of our little post-practice routine, the one we'd evolved over all the years I was just her daughter. Late that night of my homecoming I finally did get home, and I nearly wept with relief that things were exactly the same: My mom made me dinner. We ate in comfortable silence. We watched a little TV and I went to bed grateful, so incredibly grateful, that I had this safe place to come home to in any storm, the rest of my life.

My mom's home provided that sanctuary, but so did my dad's. He, too, provided me with that all-critical grounding. So did my grandpa Charlie and my brother. Not that they tried; not that they, like my mom, saw it as a mission. It's just that my success couldn't change them; nothing could. And by being totally themselves, I was able to remain, in the long-term picture, totally myself. They were a source of personal stability I could tap just by being in their presence. I could never put on airs, lose sight of who I was, as long as they breathed, because they wouldn't have tolerated it, not for a minute—they never had.

Maybe it was my grandpa Charlie's influence. He was the most genuine, most straightforward guy I ever knew. His honesty verged on the brutal. "Goddammit, Bob," he'd say to my dad, who'd cooked up a pile of brussels sprouts for dinner, "I don't know why you cook these damn things. We all HATE 'em!" One time my cousin Jeremy drove all the way to our house from the Bay Area and when he leaned down to say hi to Grandpa Charlie, my grandpa shouted, "DAMN, Jeremy! Your breath STINKS! Whaddya do, eat shit on the way down here? Go brush your teeth!"

But we loved him for that directness, all of us. It was a very comforting thing, really, because someone that direct would never lie to you, never put a shine or spin on the plain facts, never fail to tell you what other people were afraid to. You always knew where you stood, which was a very stabilizing thing indeed.

My dad, it should be noted, was the spitting image, in every way, of his father. "Don't take life too seriously," he was fond of saying—a direct quote from Grandpa Charlie—" 'cause it'll turn around and bite you in the ass." His favorite line, the one of Mae West's—"Life's a party, only most damn fools don't know they're invited"—he also got from his dad. The two of them lived their lives like a celebration, regardless of circumstance. Neither one of them altered their personalities for anyone; neither one of them could be embarrassed by anything. Not even in the presence of royalty did my dad, for instance, try to be anybody but Bob Lemme-Buy-You-a-Drink Sanders. When he was introduced to Prince Albert of Monaco during the Barcelona Games, he drew out the Prince on the topic of skiing. The whole time they were talking, they addressed each other as Dr. Sanders and Prince Albert, until finally my dad suggested they knock off the formalities. "You can call me Bob," my dad told the Prince. And then he added, "Should I call you Albert? *Or Prince Charles?*"

"A typical Bob," my mother would say later, shaking her head. Trevor and I wanted to die from embarrassment, but in a weird kind of way we were also proud of him, because he was so secure in his skin. He was totally himself with everybody, no matter how famous or rich or successful.

Because the two of them—my dad and Grandpa Charlie— were both divorced from their wives, I guess it was inevitable that my grandpa practically lived with us while we lived with my dad. Trevor and I got to know him as we might never have if my parents had stayed together. And that was truly a blessing, because my grandfather was a big part of the stability I felt growing up. He provided the stability of routine my father, in fact, did his best to avoid.

Practically every afternoon during the summer, it was Grandpa Charlie who'd pick me up from league practice. I'd be waiting for him in 110-degree heat, and he'd roll up to the curb. As soon as the door opened I'd feel this blast of icy cold air. He'd always have the air-conditioning cranked. The radio was always tuned to that great easy-listening instrumental music. The car always smelled just like Grandpa: Old Spice cologne.

Sometimes he'd take me and Trevor fishing with him. The quiet, the waiting, the heat—it's one of my sharpest memories of childhood. I have a picture of the three of us, each with a fish, my grandpa holding his with a finger through the gills. He's grinning like a fool. He loved spending time with us. He thoroughly enjoyed us. He was a comfort zone for Trevor and me all on his own.

Maybe that was the most important aspect of my sense of security: We had such a good time with each other. Not just Grandpa and me, but all my family. We had such fun doing the simplest things, my brother, my dad, my grandpa, my mom, and I, that I never had the illusion that any personal success of mine could make me any happier than I was in the company of my family. My grandpa and my dad lived to have fun, as I've described, but it was a family-wide trait—my brother and mother had it, too.

Trevor could make something as dull as a trip to the supermarket into something you wanted to be in on. We'd trail behind my mom with the cart, and while she worked through her list, we'd throw in just the grossest stuff you could find on the shelves: pickled pig's feet, or enema preparations, or facial hair bleach. Not until checkout would my mom see what it was she was buying. She'd be watching the order roll by on the conveyor, and suddenly, next to the lettuce, there'd be a plastic toilet seat cover. "Now, how did *that* get in there!" she'd blurt, genuinely surprised—as if we hadn't done this to her a million times. Trevor and I would be doubled over, and still, it would take her a few seconds. "Oh, TREVOR!" she'd say, all flustered. "Now, you take these things back *right this minute!*"

Even when my mom was mad at us for something, she never could stay mad for very long. "*Try* not to laugh," we'd say to her, with as much seriousness as we could muster. "Now— you're laughing! *Don't* laugh!" And if she didn't start laughing soon, we'd tickle her.

My mom had a real prankster side to her that even single working motherhood couldn't repress. After she remarried in 1985, we lived in a house at the end of a long lane, so that on Halloween, we hardly ever had any trick-or-treaters. It used to bum me out that no kids bothered to come to our house. So one Halloween I came home after swim practice starving, as usual, for dinner—and no one was home. I couldn't believe it. I got on the phone with my friend Heather to complain. "Can you *believe* this?" I was saying to her, when the doorbell rang. "Oh—gosh!" I said to Heather. "*Trick-or-treaters!* I gotta go!" I hung up on her, ran to open the door, and there was my mom and Steve, my stepdad—cross-dressed. She was wearing all his hunting clothes, and a mustache. He had a wig on, a lot of rouge, and these big balloon boobs. I about fell over.

And then there was that time at the Olympics. I'll never forget sitting on the bus in Barcelona, a ball of nerves because I'd qualified for the finals, and seeing, out of the corner of my eye, two women running after the bus, making a spectacle of themselves. Sure enough, it was my mom and her sister jumping up outside my window. They were frantic to get my attention. They were both wearing red shorts and stars-and-stripes T-shirts, but what caught my eye were their earrings: these glitzy masses of red, white, and blue stars, each earring so huge my mom and aunt had to hold them up as they ran so they wouldn't lose an eye.

The athletes around me turned and looked at them, and then at me, as if to say, "Do you *know* these women?" And I remember thinking, *Thank God things are never going to change in this family, no matter what happens.*

*   *   *

ALL THROUGH THAT post-Olympic period, all through the consequences of my eligibility decision, my family was my rock. I
changed; everything about my world changed; but they stayed
themselves. That stability had the subtle but critical effect of
helping me realize, my senior year, that I was finally ready to
leave not just my sport but my childhood. I was ready to be on
my own.

I realize that sounds kind of odd: Hadn't I been pretty darn
independent? Hadn't I gone to college, gone to the Olympics,
gone all over the world on my own? Yes. But I hadn't really let
go of my parents, not as my lifeline, not as my counsel, not as
the people I took for granted would cover for me, would protect
me, would fix me a meal and let me curl up on the couch and
watch a video while reporters banged on the door. Not until
December of my senior year, when I announced my retirement,
did I cut that tie.

I think what got me to that point, ironically enough, was my
eligibility decision. It had forced me to give up my scholarship.
That forced me to suddenly think about things that had been
taken care of all my life—things like health insurance, car insurance, college bills. It forced me out of the protective womb that
all serious athletes find themselves in. For years, my travel arrangements had been made, my tickets bought, my itineraries
set so that all I had to do was pack my bag, show up, and swim.
It forced me into the harsh world of making and managing
money. And that forced a certain distance on me and my parents.

I have myself to thank for setting in motion the process by

which I'd eventually leave home to strike out on my own. But I certainly have my parents to thank for giving me the tools to handle that independence, financial and otherwise.

Money was something Trevor and I knew a lot about early on. Part of it was circumstantial: living with my mom, we couldn't help but see that money was something we had to worry about. Part of it was purposeful: my dad, who'd grown up poor but had achieved quite a bit of comfort as a dentist, was emphatic about us learning how to budget our resources before we got any ideas, living with him, that money grew on trees.

In my father's house, Trevor and I were given considerable firsthand experience budgeting, even investing, money. We were in the driver's seat, spending-wise, even before we were earning it. When we turned fourteen, my father set up checking accounts for us with money for clothes, shoes, stuff we needed for school, movie tickets, and gifts. I can remember bringing home a blouse, announcing proudly that I'd bought it on sale. My dad said, "That's really nice, but how much money do you have in your account? Maybe the blouse was on sale, but it still cost money you don't have!" When we turned sixteen, we got credit cards and we were given the statements to pay off.

My dad did give us money when we really needed it. He wanted to give us the world, and if we asked him, he would. But we never took advantage of his wealth. Part of it was the example he set: My dad was very strict with himself. He was a cheapskate, in fact. He'd wear the same sweatsuit for years, and our cars, growing up, were terrible. But the thing that made us hesitate to ask him for money was that he'd make us pay—in terms of hearing out a lecture on the value of a dollar.

Every September, when it came time to buy new clothes and

shoes for school, he'd hand each of us a hundred bucks like it was some enormous chunk of change, apparently clueless that a hundred bucks would barely buy us a pair of jeans, a pair of sneakers, and a shirt. So then we had to ask him for more. And he felt obliged to give us a hard time about it. He was terribly afraid we would take money for granted if he doled it out too readily. He wanted to be sure we became long-range planners. The minute we started earning money, he made sure we saved it, and I don't mean just in a passbook savings account. Trevor wasn't even driving when he could talk knowledgeably with my dad about top-performing funds and various investment strategies.

To this day, Trevor and I dread asking our dad for money—you should have seen us planning our weddings, hoping to avoid approaching him. But I guess the real point is, he helped us quickly outgrow the need to ask him. We were on our feet, financially, long before our peers.

If my father gave us the tools to manage money for ourselves, my mother gave us the desire. She always insisted I not be dependent on anyone, as she had been until divorce forced her to regret it. Money was a constant source of tension in her life because she never had enough. She and my dad split our upbringing fifty-fifty, but they didn't bring to the task equal amounts of money. With my mother, we lived under completely different circumstances than with my father. In her house, we lived firsthand the example my father was trying to teach us by lecture.

Once her divorce was final, my mom bought a house not far from the one she and my father had built. Government housing, she called it: the roof leaked, the family room had been torn off, and instead of doors, there were these strands of beads separating our rooms from the hall—very seventies, very funky. She had no furniture to speak of, certainly not at first—just stuff she'd picked up from a flea market. For the longest time, Trevor and I slept on mattresses on the floor because she couldn't afford bedsteads and box springs.

My mother had left a home that she had helped make magazine-perfect; she was mortified having to live under these new circumstances. But Trevor and I loved that house of hers. We totally dug those seventies beads. We loved jumping on the mattresses. We thought we were the coolest of our friends, crashing on the floor every night. And we had a lot of friends in her neighborhood. We were never lonely or isolated there. What she saw as adversity, we considered an asset.

In fact, from the outset, living with my mom, we knew it didn't take money to be happy. Our very first Christmas Eve with her alone we had Big Macs for dinner—not what she had planned at all, but at the last minute our flight to my grandparents' in Omaha got canceled and, with no food at home, the only place she could afford to take us out was McDonald's. My mother was again certain she wasn't providing for us adequately; Trevor and I were in heaven.

All through those years with my mom, the littlest things made us happy. If my mom sprang for pizza and had it delivered, we'd be thrilled. One time, as a special treat, she took me to Miss Muffet's Sticker Store, a place that sold nothing but stickers by the yard, a place I'd obsessed about for some peer-influenced reason. I was beyond overjoyed when she announced I could go pick out a couple dollars' worth. It took me hours, but I finally selected a bunch of root-beer-smelling stickers—

and to this day, I remember those cheap stickers more fondly than a lot of very nice presents I've received since. I'll never forget, either, the day my mom brought home the Betamax, which some sales guy had talked her into buying over a VHS format ("It's the wave of the future," he told her). That evening, we spent hours at the video store selecting a movie, because this was so special, so important, so extraordinary. She let us pick out *Slapshot*—an R-rated movie, a real departure for my mom. We felt so treated. We were so conscious of the tight budget that ruled her days on top of the tight schedule. In contrast, I barely remember my dad bringing home his VCR. It wasn't a big deal to him financially. We took it for granted because, despite his own best advice, so did he.

My mom never understood the value of the education she gave us. She could dwell only on what she hadn't been able to give us: deluxe vacations, a backyard swimming pool, a sport court, dinners out, movies all the time. She would have loved to have been in my dad's position. To this day, she can't get it into her head that we never, ever felt deprived, living with her, that we never favored Dad just because he lived higher on the hog. We can't seem to make her see that it was her example that helped us the most: she demonstrated how a person could go from having nothing—no job skills, no safety net, no nest egg, no relatives to turn to, no moral support—to having the means to support two children and a house, the freedom to make her own life. To this day, she doesn't see her metamorphosis. But we did, growing up, and it was powerful proof of what she was always saying about getting whatever you wanted just by putting your mind to it.

Taken together, what we learned from each parent about

financial independence was all we ever needed to handle either knee-buckling adversity or mind-blowing success. We learned the value of money without ever coming to worship it. We learned what it could buy us, and we learned what it could cost us. We learned how to make it, manage it, and invest it. And we learned how to spend it: conservatively on stuff, and generously on experiences and people.

So while the wealth that came my way after the Olympics could have been my undoing—as it is the undoing of so many instant celebrities—it wasn't. It didn't succeed in clouding my priorities. Very early in my travels on the sponsorship circuit, I saw plainly what the trade-offs were going to be. The more money I made, the less time I had to enjoy what money couldn't buy: my friends, campus life, dating, biking, going for a run—the experience, in short, of being a college student, an experience I wouldn't have ever again. I decided I wanted to be rich in memories from this period, the way I'd managed to be rich in high school. So when I was offered $40,000 for yet another trip to Japan, for instance, I turned it down. I didn't want to ever make the mistake of making money at the expense of making memories. No amount of wealth, I knew, could ever make up for lost personal experience.

By THE END of 1994, a year after my momentous decision to retire, I thought I had broken free of the box that Olympic success had put me in. I was no longer swimming, but working in television. I was no longer simply Summer Sanders, That Olympic Swimmer, I was Summer Sanders, the girl who cohosted *Sandblast,* the MTV show. I had a contract in hand to tape forty more shows for MTV. I seemed to be well on my way to a new peak, in a whole new field.

But being out of swimming, down from Mt. Olympus, did not, in fact, mean I was climbing up in broadcasting. For an agonizing period of months, I didn't feel like I was even going forward, not in any direction. I had so little experience in mapping a course for myself up any mountain other than competitive swimming. Pursuing my next television job wasn't like diving in and heading in for the wall. There were no lane buoys. It most surely wasn't a straight line. I couldn't pull a no-brainer, as I had in my sport, certainly not at this point. That approach wasn't going to net me my dream of being someone like Katie Couric someday.

I could see why so many athletes stayed in their sport, or left it for something just as structured, just as mapped out. An athlete never has to worry about direction. You have a routine to perform, a finish line to reach, a wall to touch. It's so straightforward. You don't have to think. In fact, it's better if you don't. I could see why so many of my Olympic buddies either never stopped competing (Karch Kiraly, for instance) or followed the path their sponsors laid out, or went on the lecture circuit (Bonnie Blair, Matt Biondi, Dan Jansen), or went back to school (Dot Richardson, Debi Thomas, Norm Bellingham, and Justin Huish).

I'd always known, of course, that I, too, could stay in my sport or pursue some outgrowth of it and earn a decent living. But I'd majored in communications because I wanted something beyond the Games, and because I'd been raised to *not* wind up a prisoner of swimming, but to be well rounded, with plenty of options to choose from. My high-school friend

Heather and I had always wanted to be actresses: it seemed to me I'd been on one stage, and now it was time to be on another.

So, prepared as I was by both my parents and by my sport to take risks, I wallowed in transition for a while. In 1995, I was living in Los Angeles, taking everything my agent offered me, because I didn't know what I wanted, let alone how to get there. My agent would call about something involving kids, and I would be passionate—"That would be so *perfect!*" I'd say to her. "Right up my alley! I want that job so bad!"—because I did enjoy working with kids. But was that a goal? I enjoyed working in television, but did that mean I should get on a kids' television show?

I didn't know how to find my way. I didn't know what to shoot for; I didn't really know what I could do. I didn't even know who I was, hanging out with friends of my boyfriend's, working with people whose passions were completely different from mine.

My parents knew I was floundering. They knew I was unhappy—with L.A., with my job prospects, with my boyfriend. I'd call them and vent, and I knew I caused them a lot of worry; they'd never seen me like this, goal-less, direction-less, lacking in confidence. But to their enormous credit, they did not step in to break my fall, long and far as it was from what had been the top of the world. They trusted that they'd given me everything I'd need to find my way up again. They knew that what I needed most—that inner arrogance, that mental toughness, that core of certainty—they couldn't give me. Only experience could. Sooner or later, I would hit on the right one.

Coming Full Circle

When the answer came to me, the rightness of it totally took over my life. I never turned over the possibility; I never worked up to the decision. I woke up one morning and it just hit me. I remember having breakfast with my boyfriend, the two of us sitting over omelettes at our favorite brunch place.

"I'm going back to swimming," I announced. I didn't ask him, I didn't run it by him, I just told him. It was like my mouth spoke for me.

I acted on that decision with a speed that even to this day shocks me. It took me exactly one week to get a spot on the resident team in Colorado Springs, find someone to take over my apartment lease in L.A., store my furniture, pack up my truck, drive all the way to Colorado, and get back into training. Of course, I cried for three straight weeks once I'd relocated to Colorado Springs and started training. *Had I just blown every chance I ever had at a future in television? What had I done?* But I wasn't going to take it back, this decision. That was the whole idea: Face the fear. Take the risk. Whatever the outcome, you will learn from it.

It was just so clear that to get my goal-oriented, confident self back, I'd have to start pushing myself where I knew how to get results—in the pool. I had no intention of making swimming my career again, no matter how publicly successful my comeback turned out to be. My decision to return was entirely focused on getting back what, ironically enough, my success had cost me—that essential inner confidence—because I couldn't get on with my life without it.

The fear was there, big-time. I knew everybody expected I

would attain the levels I'd reached by the time I had retired, and I wasn't at all sure I could. I knew everybody would be watching me, and I wasn't at all sure I could stand that kind of scrutiny. But there was no way I could do this on the sly. By announcing to the media my plans for a comeback, by calling my coach Mike Hastings, by allowing my parents to set their sights on Atlanta, I was setting myself up for a very public trial.

Yet that was the whole challenge: not to make the Olympic team, but to not chicken out of trying. The point was to reintroduce high stakes and high goals into my life, to make striving and going all out the habit it once was so I could take it into my broadcasting career and go forward. I had learned from experience—from going all the way to the top and sliding all the way back down—that *fearing* failure was a whole lot more awful than actually failing. It had taken me more than three years, but I finally figured out I needed to face the fear or I'd never scale another mountain, not in any field.

Three years, that is, after bowing my head to receive those Olympic medals, I realized what success really was. It wasn't about getting to the top, or staying there, but about having the courage to come down and put yourself on the road to another climb.

And that's how success should be measured—not by how much money or media attention you get in one arena, but by how often and how willingly you step outside that arena to start as a nobody and flail your way to recognition again.

Of course, you can't take even the very first step toward success unless you're coming from a place of stability, security, and unconditional love. That's where parents come in. That's why the job they do early on, in terms of providing stability and support, is so important. My own parents made it easy for me to take those first steps toward an Olympic peak by attaching no particular penalty to any outcome. They made me understand I was in charge. They made me see it was all up to me. They didn't give me the dream, just the ownership of it.

That gave me the power to fulfill any potential, the tools to climb any peak. That was their success, as parents. The fact that I took that power and insisted on exploring new potential by climbing new peaks—that was my success, one far more valuable than anything people saw on television in the summer of 1992.

7

Triumph in Defeat

What is the measure of a true champion?
How she handles defeat.

Coming down the final lap of the 400 IM during the Good-will Games of 1990, I knew, I could see, I was touching first—touching out Janet Evans. Some part of me must have realized I had just vaulted into the place I'd been working toward all my life.

And yet, there at the wall, in the moment of victory—another part of me was terribly uncomfortable that my victory meant Janet's comedown. I didn't know what to do, what expression to wear on my face, so I put my arm up halfway, not fully, and when I gave a thumbs-up sign, it wasn't to the media or my coaches but to my high-school friend Heather, sitting somewhere up in the stands. That was to signify *Hey, pretty cool!*

I did a thumbs-up for the team. Then I hugged Janet.

Before the race, Rowdy Gaines, a commentator I knew, had put me through the paces of a mock news interview, just to ease the tremendous pressure I was feeling going up against Janet. He was pretending the race was over and that I had won. "What's it like beating the world's fastest woman in the 400 IM?" he had joked.

But of course, we wound up doing that interview for real. And it was so awkward, even though I'd rehearsed this very moment. I babbled like an idiot. I couldn't stop thinking how awful this was for Janet. *To lose her gold-medal event to me, an upstart, a newcomer*—God! I couldn't imagine it. She was unseated. Her reign as champion was over. *Finito.*

Yet there she stood, calmly answering Rowdy's questions, holding it together like I don't think I could have then, in her position. She could have ducked out of the interview, could have said she didn't want to talk; she could have climbed out of the pool and run off and cried or slammed her fist against a wall or any of a thousand things I've seen swimmers do after losing a big race. When Rowdy asked her what happened out there, she could have claimed some excuse, found someone or something to blame. But instead she said, "Summer swam a *great* race."

I never forgot the way she handled her defeat. Her performance during that interview confirmed the truth of that cliché about true champions. Janet certainly seemed to grasp then what it would take me years to appreciate: that the greatness of being the very best is a momentary thing, something extremely special, something to be valued and savored precisely because it is momentary. It can't possibly last, no matter how talented you are, no matter how hard you try, no matter how much you train, no matter how great your coach is, no matter how much you want it. The privilege is in having that moment at all. And Janet had the grace, there in that interview, to be grateful for the privilege, rather than bitter that it had been taken away. Where had it come from?

Six years later, at the Olympic Trials in Indianapolis, I had occasion to think of Janet all over again. I failed to qualify for the Atlanta-bound team; in the finals, I came in eighth. My gold-medal events were taken from me. And so now I really weighed my options. I could be bitterly disappointed for what I no longer had. Or I could I be grateful I'd ever had it at all.

I REMEMBER, THERE in the finals of the '96 Trials, touching the wall in the race I once "owned," the 200 butterfly. I looked back over my shoulder at the board and registered what I already knew: I wasn't even close to qualifying. I'd gone out knowing how I had to split it, how I had to be out with everybody for that first 100 meters, and I was. But my stroke looked nothing like it did in '92. I didn't have that easy speed; I felt like I was plowing the water, not skimming over the surface. Every single stroke was so . . . much . . . effort. By the second 100, I didn't think I could get my arms out of the water. I completely died. I came in a full two and half seconds behind the time I was swimming before going into the Nationals, and that was when I'd had only two months of training under my belt, not ten, as I did now.

I got out of the water and went over to Mark, my husband-to-be, who'd made the team a couple nights prior. Mark had been microphoned earlier by NBC; I turned it off. The cameras were circling me like I was roadkill. I went behind this curtain where they couldn't follow me, and tried to get a handle on what had just happened.

Total emotional turmoil. I was really mad. Sad. Surprised. Shocked. Bewildered.

Then Jim Gray of NBC poked his head in. "Summer," he said, "if you want to do an interview, now's the time, because we're about to go off the air."

I knew I wanted to talk. I wanted to explain. I thought I wanted to answer his questions, but as I did, I realized I was trying to answer my own. I didn't think about what I was saying; it just all came together, like my mouth was talking on a separate order from my brain. *Was a ten-month comeback realistic?* "Maybe ten months wasn't enough," I started to say—but even as I said it, I felt like I did when I was seven years old and tried to blame my failure on the timers. Other athletes had done it in less. *So what happened out there?*

I don't really remember the other questions. I don't think I even heard them. My answer was still going to be the same. "This is the first time I ever really appreciated what I did in 1992," I said. "It's allowed me to be proud of myself—of the shape I was in, how I swam, how tough I was, and the amazing teammates I had. I think how lucky I was to be part of such a great, awesome group of women from the '92 team. And I'm so proud of that!"

Jim said something about this being the end for me. "Yes," I said. My eyes were starting to blur; my lips were tight. I knew I was going to cry. I couldn't see pulling it together if he asked another question, so I waved goodbye and walked away, still wet, still in my suit and cap.

It dawned on me, in the course of babbling to Jim, that

maybe this just wasn't meant to be, this third run for an Olympics. The longer I talked, the more convinced I became. It just wasn't meant to be. It wasn't why I came back to swimming.

I thought back on the last ten months, training full-time at the U.S. Olympic Training Center in Colorado Springs. The more I examined it, the more I could see I had lost the race long before I'd come out and swum it. Making the next Olympic team wasn't where my heart was heading even as I put in the countless practice hours for these very Trials. One afternoon not long before the Trials I was working out on the pool deck on the biokinetic ergometer—this contraption that offers a ton of resistance to your stroke—and I remember saying to my teammates, sort of nostalgically, "This is the last time I'll be doing this." Which was true: I wouldn't be on that machine again before the Trials; if I made the team, though, I'd be back in here, at it again. "Don't say that, Summer," someone responded, thinking I was being morbid about my chances. "No, no—I didn't mean it that way!" I assured her. But in my head, even then, I wondered if maybe there was a reason I said what I said. Maybe it did mean something. Maybe it was fateful.

I knew, as I sat there discussing my training with Jim, that I wasn't going to blame not qualifying on too short a comeback period. I wasn't going to blame it on the taper process, even though I had not done it the way I should have. I wasn't keen on making excuses, to Jim or to myself. I had gone out there, given it my best, and found it wasn't enough.

After Jim said goodbye, I walked over and stood again with Mark, silently, until I'd collected myself. Then I changed into my clothes and climbed up into the stands to be with my family and my friend Heidi. My mom gave me a big hug; she'd always gauged her response by looking at my face, at my cues, and she knew better than to say anything. My dad, however, was so certain there was something wrong, that there'd been some mistake, that I was on the team. He said, "Well"—and he paused—"I'm going to Atlanta anyway!" He didn't know what to say. He was in shock. He couldn't register the fact that I'd lost. He'd rarely seen me lose.

I can remember sitting up there in the stands, exhausted, but oddly at peace. It was all over, my whole long journey to get to this place, to this moment. The Trials were over for everybody; we were just waiting for the induction ceremony, when those who had made the team would be trotted out and applauded. The arena lights went dim. The announcer boomed, "AND NOW, LADIES AND GENTLEMEN . . . ," and I saw only two familiar female faces from the '92 Olympics, Jenny and Janet, walk out and stand center stage under a sea of American flags with the other swimmers who were going to Atlanta. Looking at these newly crowned Olympians, looking at their faces, I got a huge lump in my throat. I could feel the tears welling up and burning my eyes, because I could remember the moment in '92 when I'd been down there.

But I was beginning to realize what these tears were about: I was mourning the fact that I couldn't go back to 1992 and stand down there with my buddies again and relive the anticipation, the trip to Spain, and the Games themselves, this time taking it all in, this time savoring every minute, every once-in-a-lifetime aspect, of the whole experience.

I was still upset, of course, about my own failure to make the 1996 team. I kept thinking people saw me and thought, *Ooooh, she didn't make it. . . .* It continued to shock me, the realization that I had gone out with those girls, given it everything I had, and come in eighth. It was very humbling.

Yet as I stood up there with the people I loved best, watching the 1996 team as a spectator in the stands, I thought of what my mother had said a million times over the years, before a meet: *The one who wins will be the one who wants it the most.* That was absolutely true. I hadn't wanted it enough, not in that all-consuming, totally focused way I'd had four years earlier. I had moved to Colorado Springs to confront my fear of failure, to gain confidence in life, to challenge myself again, to get that old satisfaction from applying myself to one thing and going for it. I had needed to come back to swimming in order to redis-cover what it was that made me happy, because over the last four years, taking every job that came my way, I'd lost the thread of my direction. I had come back to swimming because I needed to get the feel again of having a life with a direction. Once I got that back, I wanted to apply it to my career in television.

I could have stopped right after the Nationals. Maybe I should have: I placed in the top two after only two months of training and proved to myself I could do whatever I put my mind to.

But I didn't stop, mainly because I was really enjoying my-self. I was training for myself, swimming for myself, spending time by myself, doing what made me happy—something I hadn't had the luxury of doing since I was a kid. No conflicting agenda, no other job, no school, no rushing off to the airport, nothing but swimming as my job. I didn't see how I could not try out, after all this, for the Olympic team, even though I knew I wasn't going to top my '92 performance, and knew I wasn't going to be happy about that. I felt I had to try out and make the team to save face. But I never visualized myself going to Atlanta. That just wasn't part of the picture.

When the ceremonies were over and everybody had gone home, two of my former Olympic teammates and I went out to a brewery together and ate and talked, not about my failing to make the team but about all that had led up to this night: all the memories we'd had growing up swimming, all the fun we'd had on away meets, the tremendous high of being at the very top of our sport during the NCAAs, and the emotional roller coaster we'd been on during those weeks in Barcelona. It was all there for the savoring, all there waiting for me to be completely done with trying to swim faster and faster. Now I could step back and revel in what I'd seen, and done, and felt, and experienced. I'd had an incredible career. A nineteen-year string of awesome experiences. A member of the United States Swimming Team at the age of fifteen. Full scholarship to Stanford. Three Goodwill Games gold medals. World Champion in 200 butterfly. Four-time American record holder. Six individual and one team NCAA titles. Four Olympic medals.

I had worked hard, and I'd been rewarded. I'd given my best, and for a while, my best was the best in the world. I appreciated everything—my sport, my teammates, my friends, my coaches, my brother, my parents. I sat there and soaked up the satisfaction, enjoying all the success I'd never been able to stop long enough to really feel. I could take pride in all that I'd achieved, take stock of where I was and what had gotten me there, and take charge of where I was going.

By then, my entire family showed up, worried that I was still in shock, still hurting. I wasn't; I truly wasn't. We ordered a round of shots at the bar. Everybody downed them, and then we all danced.

After that night, people would come up to me and say, "You know, you should give it another try, Summer. End on a good note!"

Which I find so ironic. Because back in December of 1993, when I formally retired from swimming, my times were terrific—but I didn't feel I was ending on a good note because I wasn't having any fun. I had retired because I'd gotten totally fed up with my life as a professional swimmer. That wasn't closure. Not loving my sport was *not* how I wanted to end my career.

But to be sitting with my friends Nicole and Janie, hours after my very public failure, and loving—*loving*—swimming, for all that it had given me, and for all that I felt I was taking from it and applying in my new career—*this* was ending on a good note.

I'M NOT TRYING to suggest defeat is some ennobling thing. It's hard. It hurts like hell.

"That feeling you'll never be in that type of arena again—with the pressure, the excitement, everything that goes into the Olympics," Dan Jansen told me, "it's an adjustment for every athlete. You realize you're never going to be the best in the world at another thing. You have to accept it—and let it go."

Stepping down from the very top is even harder. But I didn't feel bitter. I came home from the Trials extremely conscious of, and grateful for, what my sport and my parents had given me. Because the Trials were, ultimately, a test of everything my parents had believed in, a test of the job they had done preparing me for an entire lifetime of ups and downs. Was I going to look backward the rest of my life, to that brief moment on top of the world as a swimmer? Or was my success as a swimmer just the beginning, just the launch I'd need to go forward into anything I chose?

If they hadn't had the right values, the right emphases, the right philosophy on parenting—if they had ever subscribed to the notion that Making a Child Number One is the end that justifies any means—then the outcome of the Trials would have indeed spelled total failure for me. I would be doomed to spend the rest of my life bitter, for sure; I would be like those athletes all of us know, thanks to the media's fascination with them, who never lose gracefully—because they simply cannot *afford* to lose. Winning *is* everything, for them, because it always *has* been everything. They've never developed interests or abilities outside of their sport, or they were never encouraged to, or, as children, they were never allowed to. Other sports, other activities, school stuff, parties, vacations, friendships, family life—everything was sacrificed to the goal of being number one in their sport.

Those athletes surely do have reason to be bitter in defeat.

The fact that I had a network of friends and family with whom I shared concrete memories of events and moments to-tally outside of swimming—people who would say, for years and years to come, "Remember when we did . . . ?"—that was the key to handling both mind-blowing success and mas-sively public defeat. What made all the difference, that fateful final night at the '96 Trials, was exactly what had made all the difference that fateful final afternoon at the '92 Olympics: I could shrug off the pressure of winning or losing just by thinking about the people with whom I shared incredible memories, memories I'd never been denied by reason of being a swimmer, memories of experiences more golden than any medal in my sock drawer. For days, weeks, months after my defeat at the Trials, I reviewed those memory tapes, incredibly grateful that my parents had never allowed my sport to do anything but expand my circle of friends and experiences. Because in reviewing all I'd done outside of swimming, I found I'd had a full life. I'd missed out on nothing I didn't choose to miss out on.

I didn't feel dread looking forward, either: I didn't think, *My life is effectively over.* The Olympics were a pinnacle, yes—but of my nineteenth year, of my swimming career, not of my life. Defeat allowed me to shift my focus to other ascents. It's true what Norm Bellingham says: it's tough to travel to the next peak when you see you're at the bottom, after being at the top. But you quickly realize *you know how to pursue excellence.* It's still a climb, but you'll climb it faster, because you know how to work hard and stay focused.

There's something to be said, too, Norm adds, for having to make those steps sooner, rather than later.

"You think if you place first, you'll purge all those demons of self-doubt," he says. "But, in fact, you're only postponing the confrontation. Because when you're lionized by the press, you're not critical of yourself. You're not improving. You're not learning. You're losing precious years in learning how to deal with all the problems life doles out."

Our parents understood this, says Dan Jansen, speaking for all of us Olympians. They made us aware there'd be a time when our athletic career would end, and no matter how high our achievement, life would still have its ups and downs.

Dan never saw his parents' contribution more clearly than the day his sister died. His mom had not come to Calgary for Dan's performance; she had told Dan a week earlier, when he was made World Champion in his hometown, that she didn't feel right about leaving Jane at that time. His dad, though, did go to Calgary to be with Dan. Only the night before Dan's race, when his mom called to report that Jane had taken a turn for the worse, did he leave Dan to be with her.

"I felt guilty that my dad even came," Dan recalls, "but for my parents to have made the decision to split this—to have one stay with Jane, and one come with me—that's when I thought, *How really great they are, to have the selflessness to do that in order to support two of us in completely different struggles.*

"Who they were as people," Dan adds, "that's what they gave us."

I'd have to agree. My parents' focus was always on raising Trevor and me to be decent human beings, people who would one day be in a position to give back—people, as Dot Richardson puts it, who would leave the world a better place than they found it. To that end, they parented best by example: they gave freely and joyfully of all they had to give in the way of support and encouragement without the slightest expectation of "payback" from us.

My dad is still baffled by parents' confusion on this issue. They'll ask him, "Gee, Bob, your kids turned out so incredibly well. How did you do it?"

"It's so simple!" I've heard him answer in that guileless way of his. "You love your kids? Spend time with them! *Enjoy* them!"

EPILOGUE

Giving Back

S ome months after the '96 Olympic Trials, I went to the Nationals to watch my husband-to-be, Mark Henderson, compete. Naturally, people came up to me; it had been my arena, my sport, my stage for so long, I couldn't possibly expect to be anonymous. And of course, they all asked me what I was doing with my life.

For any ex-Olympian, that's usually *the* killer question. You feel you have to have something great to tell them. If you've been an Olympic champion and you come in with a job that doesn't impress people, or no job at all, or "Gee . . . I'm not really sure what's next," people will talk. I knew just how people talked. Actually, I didn't *really* know, but I imagined them analyzing me, almost waiting to see me fail. That was the image I had, the feeling I had when I went back to a swim meet and I was asked questions about what I was doing—like it was a test. I imagined they were wondering things like *Has she gained weight? Or what's keeping her from being at the top of her sport?*

But I felt I could walk into that sports arena where my fiancé was competing—where I had competed just a year earlier, and placed second—with my head held high, because my credentials outside the pool area were getting to be just as impressive as what they'd been in it. I didn't shrink from people's questions one tiny bit. Just hearing myself respond—"Well, I'm hosting a show on Nickelodeon, I'm working with the NBA, and I'm a sideline reporter with the WNBA. . . ."

Even I felt like *Wow! I've made the transition! I'm meeting brand-new challenges, brand-new goals!*

And that realization made me feel grateful all over again for the kind of upbringing I'd been given: one where I was taught to embrace experience, use it to make my own decisions, and above all, live through the consequences of those decisions.

That's what prompted me to want to write this book. I'd been given so much, by my parents, my coaches, my teammates, I wanted to thank them—and at the same time, I wanted to give other kids what I'd been given, by sharing with their parents what my parents did right. I wanted my parents' example to be out there, to be an inspiration.

Because we all learn best, I think, by example.

Recently I was talking to an athlete I know who'd auditioned for the host spot on a television show. She'd just found out she was among the top three candidates being considered.

"And I have *you* to thank," she said.

I had no idea what she was talking about.

" 'Cause, you know," she went on, "they're looking for the Summer Sanders thing."

She was looking at me the way I look at Donna DeVarona, the swimmer from the late sixties who, after participating in two Olympics, was the first female to sign a sports commentator contract with ABC. She had to end her athletic career at the age of seventeen because back then there were no college athletic programs for women—an inequality she helped change for my generation. Donna, in fact, *is* Ms. Title Nine, the change that made college competition available to women. She's also one of the founders of the Women in Sports Foundation. In every respect, she was the trailblazer, and it was her example that inspired my career choice.

Yet it's my example, surprisingly, that the next crop of Olympic athletes are noticing. One girl told my agent that she, too, "wanted to go the Summer Sanders route." I'm a transitional breed, as Dot Richardson puts it: by following Donna DeVarona, and trying to take what she did one step further, I'm showing the women who follow me that this is how we pay our debt to pioneers like Donna. We honor their accomplishment by playing the game and playing it even better.

I have to say, I'm very honored that someone wants to go my route, even go faster and farther than me. It's the same feeling I get when I talk to a group of kids: that it would be kind of cool if I left them with something that might really give them inspiration and hope. I want to leave them saying to themselves, "I wanna do that! I *can* do that! I want to be even better than that!" I've always had this all-empowering belief that there are no closed doors, no barriers that cannot be broken through; that if I want something badly enough—if I can just visualize it or have it shown to me—then it's within my reach, and I have the power to make it happen for myself. I want them to have it.

Giving Back

*   *   *

I CAN'T WAIT to have kids, even though I've told Mark, "We'll
open that discussion in 2000." When we do have kids, I want
them to know Mark and me as individuals, as well as a parental
unit. I hope that's possible. I'm forever sad that I don't have one
single memory of my parents as a team, as a unit, living together
in our house, but I couldn't be more grateful that I know
everything there is to know about each of them. Neither one
ever had the option of shielding us from their sad moments,
their bad moments, their tears or worries; Trevor and I knew
our parents as human beings, capable of making mistakes but
finding a way to enjoy life, and enjoy us, regardless. My dad
always insisted on living life as a celebration, but my mom loved
a good time, too, which is why I always preferred her company
even to my friends when we had a chance to go out. (I don't
know anybody but my mom who would want to go out to
dinner, go out to a comedy club, and then want to go out
dancing until all hours.)

I think that's the highest compliment I could pay my parents: I would often rather go to a movie or spend time with
them than with anyone else. We loved each other's company.
Laughter was a constant whether I was living with my dad or
my mom. Neither one of my parents got preoccupied with
scolding, or punishing, or being mad at us. It was clear to
Trevor and me that our parents would much rather enjoy every
minute they had with us, because they didn't have all that
many. We would be children for only so many years.

I only hope Mark and I will have the same attitude of joy
toward our children.